CAROLINA MARIA DE JESUS

is a Brazilian woman with only two years of schooling, the mother of three illegitimate children, each born of a different father. This story of her life in São Paulo explodes as a vivid, incendiary social document.

With fierce and stark simplicity Carolina tells of her filthy house in the favela and the equally squalid homes of her neighbors. She describes the gnawing hunger that invades every shack, that drives her to hunt for paper and scraps of metal that will bring just enough money to keep her and her children alive. Her story is a witness to the vicious fights, the knifings, the sordid sex life of the *favelados* —prisoners of poverty, prey of the unscrupulous, breeders of revolution.

"It is both an ugly book and a touchingly beautiful book. It carries protest and it carries compassion. There is even bitter humor. As a fast-paced and strangely observant account of sheer misery, Child of the Dark is an immensely disturbing study of what can happen to a segment of the population of one of the world's potentially wealthiest nations. . . . A rarely matched essay on the meaning and the feeling of hunger, degradation, and want."

—*New York Times Book Review*

Studies in Sociology from MENTOR and SIGNET CLASSIC

(0451)

☐ **THE PLEASURES OF SOCIOLOGY edited by Lewis A. Coser.** Sociology comes alive in this collection of thirty-six of the clearest, most stimulating writings in the field. With a combination of deep insight and excellent literary style, some of the greatest sociological thinkers come to grips with the most enduring questions about the individual and society. Introduction by the editor. With a list of suggested additional readings. (622642—$4.50)*

☐ **URBAN LEGACY: The Story of America's Cities by Diana Klebanow, Franklin L. Jonas and Ira M. Leonard.** A vivid history of American cities from colonial times to the '70s. *Urban Legacy* traces the progressive urbanization and suburbanization of American society and the impact of urbanism upon American life, including unemployment, the flight to the suburbs, bankruptcy and crime. Illustrations. Maps. Bibliography. Political Cartoons.
(615867—$2.95)

☐ **A WELFARE MOTHER by Susan Sheehan.** The profile of a New York City welfare mother: her life with various "husbands" and her nine children. A moving account of the culture of poverty. "This is life on its own terms . . . a fine achievement, a perfect book . . . should be read!"—*Saturday Review.* Winner of a Sidney Hillman award for innovative reporting on a social problem. Introduction by Michael Harrington. (619498—$2.25)

☐ **TWENTY YEARS AT HULL HOUSE by Jane Addams.** Foreword by Henry Steele Commager. A graphic account of the famed Chicago settlement house from 1889–1909. Bibliography, Biographical Note, drawings, index and photographs included. (515641—$2.50)

*Price slightly higher in Canada

Buy them at your local bookstore or use this convenient coupon for ordering.

THE NEW AMERICAN LIBRARY, INC.,
P.O. Box 999, Bergenfield, New Jersey 07621
Please send me the books I have checked above. I am enclosing $_____
(please add $1.00 to this order to cover postage and handling). Send check or money order—no cash or C.O.D.'s. Prices and numbers are subject to change without notice.
Name_____
Address_____
City _____ State _____ Zip Code _____
Allow 4-6 weeks for delivery.
This offer is subject to withdrawal without notice.

CHILD *of the* DARK

The DIARY of
CAROLINA MARIA DE JESUS

Translated from the Portuguese
by DAVID ST. CLAIR

Illustrated with Photographs

A MENTOR BOOK
NEW AMERICAN LIBRARY
TIMES MIRROR

ENGLISH TRANSLATION COPYRIGHT © 1962 BY E. P. DUTTON,
CO., INC., NEW YORK, AND SOUVENIR PRESS, LTD., LONDON

All rights reserved. No part of this book may be reproduced in
any form without permission in writing from the publisher,
except by a reviewer who wishes to quote brief passages in
connection with a review written for inclusion in a magazine,
newspaper or broadcast. For information address E. P. Dutton, Inc.,
2 Park Avenue, New York, New York 10016.

*This is an authorized reprint of a hardcover edition published
by E. P. Dutton, Inc.*

Published in the Portuguese language as *Quarto de Despejo*
by Livraria Francisco Alves, 1960

MENTOR TRADEMARK REG. U.S. PAT. OFF. AND FOREIGN COUNTRIES
REGISTERED TRADEMARK—MARCA REGISTRADA
HECHO EN CHICAGO, U.S.A.

SIGNET, SIGNET CLASSIC, MENTOR, PLUME, MERIDIAN AND NAL
BOOKS *are published by The New American Library, Inc.,
1633 Broadway, New York, New York 10019*

11   12   13   14   15   16   17   18   19

PRINTED IN THE UNITED STATES OF AMERICA

ILLUSTRATIONS

TRANSLATOR'S PREFACE

"*July 15, 1955.* The birthday of my daughter Vera Eunice. I wanted to buy a pair of shoes for her, but the price of food keeps us from realizing our desires. Actually we are slaves to the cost of living. I found a pair of shoes in the garbage, washed them, and patched them for her to wear."

Thus begins this book, the diary of a simple uneducated slum Negress that has been called by critics "possibly one of the best books to come from a Brazilian in this century."

Carolina is a product of her time and is acutely aware of the time and the way her life is moving. She writes of contemporary society and its impact around her. She has not tried to be artistic—just sincere.

Brazil is a modern paradox. Discovered by the Portuguese sea captain Pedro Álvares Cabral in 1500 (just eight years after Columbus), the land was turned into a colony of the King, who promptly started taking things out of it rather than putting things in. Not as ruthless as the Spanish in Peru (possibly because there were no golden Inca-like cities), the Portuguese merely put the Indians to work on their huge sugar and cocoa plantations. Spices and rich woods had to be exported to luxury-loving Lisbon, and when the Indians died off because of the heavy work, Portugal raided the coast of Africa and brought in thousands of Negro slaves.

The colony prospered and the shoreline sprang up with cities rich with gilt churches and baroque slave blocks. When the emperor Dom João VI decided to move the capital from easily sacked Bahia to Rio de Janeiro in 1763, the wealth and the culture moved with him.

But it was always along the coast. The interior remained virgin and unexploited. There were those that looked for rubber along the banks of the Amazon, or those that dug diamonds and amethysts in Minas Gerais, but Brazil was too big (actually larger than the continental United States) and what little industry was available settled into easy living along the pleasant tropical coast.

Slaves were freed in 1888 and Brazil became a republic with equal rights for all. Equal rights and freedom meant the Negro had to work for his daily ration of beans and rice, and the work was in the cities.

But the work wasn't there. Not for all of them anyway, and those who couldn't find work settled on low unwanted swamplands in São Paulo or on high hills in Rio and built their shacks. Thus the *favelas,* the slums, began.

The north of Brazil is dry. When the great droughts hit every two years or so, hundreds die of thirst. Cattle wander in circles looking for water and their rotting carcasses are picked apart by the vultures. The northern farmer (*nordestino*) sees his family decimated. He remembers tales of famine and abject poverty from his father and grandfather. So when the droughts hit he bundles his family and his few possessions into an open truck and takes the long hot dusty journey to Rio or São Paulo. There, there should be work. There, there should be abundant food and water. There, there should be opportunity.

There is. But not for the uneducated and unskilled. Shops and offices will not hire a man who cannot write his own name or speak correct Portuguese. Factories can't be bothered with illiterate men who have only agricultural experience, and it takes too long to train them. So the distraught father looks around for a place to put his family until things get better. He has no money. He has no friends. He finds a place in a favela. In Rio there are 200 favelas with a population of 337,500 souls, a 99 per cent increase over the 1950 census. In São Paulo (where work has been more plentiful these past few years) there are only seven favelas, with 50,000 living there. They grow and grow and grow until they are small cities of filth, perversion, and prostitution.

The local governments do nothing about them. Some churches and charities try to help but the problem is staggering and heartbreaking. Each year more and more people are forced to the favelas as they search for work in the cities. Erasing the cancerous growths is not the answer. It would be like trying to kill a tree by pulling off its leaves. The real solution is industrialization of the underdeveloped areas, so the distraught fathers would not have to come to the cities in the first place.

Politicians make big promises to the *favelados*. They're going to do all sorts of things if elected. But once elected they forget about their problem children and spend their time thinking of pleasanter things.

This breeds discontent among the people. And discontent breeds Communism. Middle- and upper-class Brazilians look with growing fear upon this powerful mass of the hungry in the heart of their two richest cities. If there should appear a Brazilian Fidel Castro, and if he should give these hungry illiterates guns . . .

Carolina Maria de Jesus came to the favela of Canindé in 1947. She was unemployed and pregnant. No one wanted her. Her lover had abandoned her and the white family where she worked as a maid refused to let her in the house. She was desperate and turned to the favela. Carrying boards on her head from the construction site of a church five miles away, she built a shack, roofed it with flattened tin cans and cardboard. Three months later her son João was born. Then began the fight for survival that only ceased with the publication of her diary.

Carolina was born in 1913 in the little town of Sacramento in the state of Minas Gerais, in the interior of Brazil. Her mother, an unmarried farm hand, was worried about her daughter having the same kind of life and insisted that Carolina attend school. The little girl hated it, and every morning her mother practically had to spank her all the way to the one-room building. It was only when she learned to read, three months after opening day, that she enjoyed her education.

"It was a Wednesday, and when I left school I saw a paper with some writing on it. It was an announcement of the local movie house. 'Today. Pure Blood. Tom Mix.'

"I shouted happily—'I can read! I can read!' "

She wandered through the streets reading aloud the labels in the drugstore window and the names of the stores.

For the next two years Carolina was first in her class. Then her mother got a better job on a farm far away from Sacramento and Carolina had to give up her beloved school. She never went back. Her education stopped at the second grade.

Her first days in the country were spent crying, but

with time she began to appreciate the beauties of nature: trees, birds, creeks, silence. The miracle of seeds especially intrigued the girl. But when she was completely at home in the country her mother moved again, this time to the city of Franca near São Paulo. Carolina was sixteen years old. She got a job in a hospital, ran away to sing in a circus, sold beer and cleaned hotel rooms. Then she wandered to the big city of São Paulo. She slept under bridges and in doorways, until she got a job as maid in a white family. "But I was too independent and didn't like to clean up their messes. Besides I used to slip out of the house at night and make love. After four months they fired me." Six more jobs and six more dismissals ended with the discovery that she was pregnant. "He was a Portuguese sailor, and he got on his ship fast when I told him I was going to have a baby."

Carolina built her shack like the others there. When it rained the water came in the roof, rotting her one mattress and rusting the few pots and pans. There was a sack over the window that she'd pull for privacy and late at night she would light a small kerosene lamp "and cover my nose with a rag to take away some of the favela stench."

With a baby she couldn't get work. He had to be looked after constantly. She heard that junk yards paid for scrap paper and so, strapping her tiny son to her back, she walked the streets of rich São Paulo looking for trash. She filled a burlap bag with everything she could find, and foraged in rich houses' garbage cans for bits of food and old clothes. Usually by noon she would have enough paper to sell. She got one cruzeiro (about one-fourth of a U.S. cent) per pound. "On good days I would make twenty-five or thirty cents. Some days I made nothing."

Carolina was attractive and liked men and so two years later a Spaniard "who was white and gave me love and money" went back to Europe and her second son José Carlos was born. Life continued as it was, collecting paper, ransacking garbage cans, but now with two children clinging to her. In 1943 "I met a rich white man who thought I was pretty. I would visit him and he would give me food and money to buy clothes for my sons. He didn't know for a long time that I bore his daughter. He has many servants and I guess that's where Vera Eunice gets her fancy ways."

With three children to raise life became torture. "How

horrible it is to see your children eat and then ask: 'Is there more?' This word 'more' bounces inside a mother's head as she searches the cooking pot knowing there isn't any more."

In order to keep from thinking about her troubles she started to write. Poems, novels, plays, "anything and everything, for when I was writing I was in a golden palace, with crystal windows and silver chandeliers. My dress was finest satin and diamonds sat shining in my black hair. Then I put away my book and the smells came in through the rotting walls and rats ran over my feet. My satin turned to rags and the only things shining in my hair were lice."

After a day of carrying paper her arms and back would ache so that she couldn't sleep. "I would lie on the bed and start to worry about the next day. I knew there was no bread in the house and that Vera needed a pair of shoes. I was so nervous about my children that many times I'd vomit, but there was nothing there but bile. Then I'd get up, light the lamp, and write." Her notebooks were those she found in the trash, writing on the clean side of the page with a treasured fountain pen, making slow even letters.

Her neighbors knew of her writings and made fun of them. Most of them couldn't even read, but thought she should be doing other things with her spare time than writing and saving old notebooks. They called her "Dona" (Madame) Carolina. Because of her standoffish ways she was accused of causing trouble, sleeping with everyone's husband, and calling the police each time there was a fight. Her children were stoned and charged with stealing by the neighbors. Once in a jealous rage, because Carolina wouldn't attend a drunken party-orgy, a woman filed a complaint against her son João, who was then eleven, claiming he had raped her two-year-old daughter. Carolina's life was miserable but she refused to lower the standards she had set for herself and her children and mingle with those she couldn't stand.

She had as little as possible to do with her neighbors. She hated standing at the city-installed water spigot waiting to fill her can and hated haggling with the *favelado* who had the only electric line in the section and made a living running wires from his box to neighbors' shacks and illegally charging for the electricity.

In April of 1958, Audalio Dantas, a young reporter, was covering the inauguration of a playground near Canindé for his newspaper. When the politicians had made their speeches and gone away, the grown men of the favela began fighting with the children for a place on the teeter-totters and swings. Carolina, standing in the crowd, shouted furiously: "If you continue mistreating these children, I'm going to put all your names in my book!"

Interested, the reporter asked the tall black woman about her book. At first she didn't want to talk to him, but slowly he won her confidence and she took him to her shack. There in the bottom drawer of a dilapidated dresser she pulled out her cherished notebooks. The first ones she showed him were fiction—tales of kings and princesses, plays about the fancy rich, and poems about the forest and open countryside. They were crude, childlike works, much like a primitive painting done in words. After more prodding, Dantas got her to admit that she was writing a diary. He sat on the floor reading avidly the daily notations until Carolina had to light the lamp. Enthused, he told her he wanted to show her diary to a publisher, but she told him: "I didn't write it for anyone to see. It is filled with ugly things and ugly people. Maybe after I die it will be published, but not now."

Dantas persuaded her to let him take one of the note-books—there were twenty-six of them covering a three-year span—to his newspaper. And the next day while the story on the playground got small notice, a two-column full-length excerpt from Carolina's diary appeared.

The story electrified the town. People telephoned and stopped by the newspaper office asking if there was going to be more. "Even my cynical newspaper cronies were interested," says Dantas, "and felt it should be published. Some thought it should be cleaned up a bit, as there were some rough remarks and unkind political comments, but others thought all it needed was editing." Then, as with all newspaper stories, the furore died down.

Shortly after this Dantas was offered the important position of chief of the São Paulo bureau of *O Cruzeiro* magazine, Brazil's biggest weekly. Here, he saw an even better opportunity to bring the story of Carolina's life to the attention of all Brazilians. For one full year he worked on her notebooks, ignoring the childlike novels, and concentrating on her diary, extracting the best of each day. It took a great deal of convincing on his part to get her to agree to publish excerpts from her account of her daily life. She wanted her short stories and poems published first Dantas, with his sharp reporter's mind, saw the value and the urgency of her diary, and soon she was working on it and nothing else.

After almost a lifetime in the favela she was not used to kindness from anyone and there were times when she distrusted what he was doing for her, and refused to talk to him or give up the precious manuscripts. Then sometimes he would visit and she'd put a fresh ribbon in her hair and write "Viva Audalio" on the walls of the shack.

As Carolina is a perfectionist she started every entry telling what time she got up, what she did before she went out to gather paper, and what she saw in the streets. Most of this was repetitious and Dantas cut savagely until he got the diary down to its present size. "But I did not rewrite," he insists. "The words and ideas are Carolina's. All I did was edit."

Published, her diary became the literary sensation of Brazil. Over a thousand people swamped the bookshop on the first day of sales. (In Brazil book publishers have their own retail shops; the publisher of *Quarto de Despejo* had a publication day autographing party at his shop, and did not release the book to other booksellers for one week.) Carolina signed 600 copies that afternoon, and would have done more if she hadn't stopped to talk to each of the buyers. She asked what their names were, where they lived, and if they were happy. When a state senator appeared with flash bulbs popping, Carolina wrote in his book: "I hope that you give the poor people what they need and stop putting all the tax money into your own pocket. Sincerely, Carolina Maria de Jesus."

Never had a book such an impact on Brazil. In three days the first printing of 10,000 copies was sold out in São Paulo alone. In less than six months 90,000 copies were sold in Brazil and today it is still on the best-seller list, having sold more than any other Brazilian book in history.

Carolina was invited to speak about the favela problem on radio and television, and she gave lectures on the problem in Brazilian universities. Her book has become required reading in sociology classes and the São Paulo Law University has given her the title of "Honorary Member," the first such person so honored who has not a university education. The title was originally slated for Jean Paul Sartre, but the students decided that Carolina was "far worthier in the fight for freedom" than the French philosopher.

Two months after the publication of the diary Carolina loaded her table, two small beds and a mattress, a closet, a bookshelf, six pots, herself and her children into the back of an open truck and prepared to leave the favela that she had lived in for twelve years. She had used the first proceeds from the book for the down payment on a brick house in the suburbs. But the neighbors had other ideas. They swarmed around the truck and wouldn't let her leave. "You think you are high class now, don't you, you black whore," shouted one man. "You write about us and make lots of money and then leave without sharing it."

Carolina refused to reply.

"You wrote bad things about me," shouted a drunken skinny woman named Leila. "You did worse things than I did." And with this she hurled a rock that hit young José Carlos on the cheek, making a deep gash and causing blood to flow. Others started to scream and throw stones. Vera was struck in the back and on the arm, while Carolina tried to shield her with her body. She beat on the hood of the truck and the driver roared through the crowd, who came surging behind with sticks and rotten vegetables. They chased the truck as far as the police station, then fell away.

Carolina is not really the main personage in her diary. It is a bigger character—Hunger. From the first to the last page he appears with an unnerving consistency. The other characters are consequences of this Hunger: alcoholism, prostitution, violence, and murder. The human beings who walk through these pages are real, with their real names, but with slight variations they could be other men who live with Hunger in New York, Buenos Aires, Rome, Calcutta, and elsewhere.

Carolina's words are the words of the street. Her Portuguese is not the flowing classical language spoken by the upper classes, but the short choppy urgent speech of the poor. She wasn't taught in school to make paragraphs or to be consistent with her tenses. None of this has been altered in the translation, for to do it would be to alter the woman herself. She writes directly, roughly, and without artifice. She recorded what she saw in such a way that she makes the reader feel it too. No small feat.

Recently on a television program a well-dressed, well-fed Carolina said: "If I wasn't so happy I would cry. When I first gave my manuscript to Brazilian editors they laughed at this poor Negro woman with calloused hands who wore rags and only had two years of schooling. They told me I should write on toilet paper. Now these same editors are asking for my works, actually fighting for them.

"Today I had lunch in a wonderful restaurant and a photographer took my picture. I told him: 'Write under the photo that Carolina who used to eat from trash cans now eats in restaurants. That she has come back into the human race and out of the Garbage Dump.' "

DAVID ST. CLAIR

Rio de Janeiro
  January 1962.

The DIARY of
CAROLINA MARIA DE JESUS

1955

July 15, 1955 The birthday of my daughter Vera Eunice. I wanted to buy a pair of shoes for her, but the price of food keeps us from realizing our desires. Actually we are slaves to the cost of living. I found a pair of shoes in the garbage, washed them, and patched them for her to wear.

I didn't have one cent to buy bread. So I washed three bottles and traded them to Arnaldo. He kept the bottles and gave me bread. Then I went to sell my paper. I received 65 cruzeiros. I spent 20 cruzeiros for meat. I got one kilo of ham and one kilo of sugar and spent six cruzeiros on cheese. And the money was gone.

I was ill all day. I thought I had a cold. At night my chest pained me. I started to cough. I decided not to go out at night to look for paper. I searched for my son João. He was at Felisberto de Carvalho Street near the market. A bus had knocked a boy into the sidewalk and a crowd gathered. João was in the middle of it all. I poked him a couple of times and within five minutes he was home.

I washed the children, put them to bed, then washed myself and went to bed. I waited until 11:00 for a certain someone. He didn't come. I took an aspirin and laid down again. When I awoke the sun was sliding in space. My daughter Vera Eunice said: "Go get some water, Mother!" *July 16* I got up and obeyed Vera Eunice. I went to get the water. I made coffee. I told the children that I didn't have any bread, that they would have to drink their coffee plain and eat meat with *farinha*.[1] I was feeling ill and decided to cure myself. I stuck my finger down my throat twice, vomited, and knew I was under the evil eye. The upset feeling left and I went to Senhor Manuel, carrying some cans to sell. Everything that I find in the garbage I sell. He gave me 13 cruzeiros. I kept thinking that I had to buy bread, soap, and milk for Vera Eunice. The 13 cruzeiros wouldn't make it. I returned home, or rather to my shack, nervous and exhausted. I thought of the worrisome life that I led. Carrying paper, washing clothes for the children, staying in the street all day long. Yet I'm always lacking things, Vera doesn't have shoes and she doesn't like to go barefoot. For at least two years I've wanted to buy a meat grinder. And a sewing machine.

I came home and made lunch for the two boys. Rice, beans, and meat, and I'm going out to look for paper. I left the children, told them to play in the yard and not go into the street, because the terrible neighbors I have won't leave my children alone. I was feeling ill and wished I could lie down. But the poor don't rest nor are they permitted the pleasure of relaxation. I was nervous inside, cursing my luck. I collected two sacks full of paper. Afterward I went back and gathered up some scrap metal, some cans, and some kindling wood. As I walked I thought—when I return to the favela there is going to be something new. Maybe Dona Rosa or the insolent Angel Mary fought with my children. I found Vera Eunice sleeping and the boys playing in the street. I thought: it's 2:00. Maybe I'm going to get through this day without anything happening. João told me that the truck that gives out money was here to give out food. I took a sack and hurried out. It was the leader of the Spiritist Center at 103 Vergueiro Street. I got two kilos of rice, two of beans, and two kilos of macaroni. I was happy. The truck went away. The nervousness that I had inside left me. I took advantage of my calmness to read. I picked up a magazine and sat on the grass, letting the rays of the sun warm me as I read a story. I wrote a note and gave it to my boy João to take to Senhor Arnaldo to buy soap, two aspirins, and some bread. Then I put water on the stove to make coffee. João came back saying

---

[1] *Farinha:* a coarse wheat flour.

he had lost the aspirins. I went back with him to look. We didn't find them.

When I came home there was a crowd at my door. Children and women claiming José Carlos had thrown stones at their houses. They wanted me to punish him.

July 17 Sunday A marvelous day. The sky was blue without one cloud. The sun was warm. I got out of bed at 6:30 and went to get water. I only had one piece of bread and three cruzeiros. I gave a small piece to each child and put the beans, that I got yesterday from the Spiritist Center, on the fire. Then I went to wash clothes. When I returned from the river the beans were cooked. The children asked for bread. I gave the three cruzeiros to João to go and buy some. Today it was Nair Mathias who started an argument with my children. Silvia and her husband have begun an open-air spectacle. He is hitting her and I'm disgusted because the children are present. They heard words of the lowest kind. Oh, if I could move from here to a more decent neighborhood!

I went to Dona Florela to ask for a piece of garlic. I went to Dona Analia and got exactly what I expected: "I don't have any!"

I went to collect my clothes. Dona Aparecida asked me: "Are you pregnant?"

"No, Senhora," I replied gently.

I cursed her under my breath. If I am pregnant it's not your business. I can't stand these favela women, they want to know everything. Their tongues are like chicken feet. Scratching at everything. The rumor is circulating that I am pregnant! If I am, I don't know about it!

I went out at night to look for paper. When I was passing the São Paulo football stadium many people were coming out. All of them were white and only one black. And the black started to insult me:

"Are you looking for paper, auntie? Watch your step, auntie dear!"

I was ill and wanted to lie down, but I went on. I met several friends and stopped to talk to them. When I was going up Tiradentes Avenue I met some women. One of them asked me:

"Are your legs healed?"

After I was operated on, I got better, thanks to God. I could even dance at Carnival in my feather costume. Dr.

José Torres Netto was who operated on me. A good doctor. And we spoke of politics. When a woman asked me what I thought of Carlos Lacerda,[2] I replied truthfully:

"He is very intelligent, but he doesn't have an education. He is a slum politician. He likes intrigues, to agitate."

One woman said it was a pity, that the bullet that got the major didn't get Carlos Lacerda.

"But his day . . . it's coming," commented another.

Many people had gathered and I was the center of attention. I was embarrassed because I was looking for paper and dressed in rags. I didn't want to talk to anyone, because I had to collect paper. I needed the money. There was none in the house to buy bread. I worked until 11:30. When I returned home it was midnight. I warmed up some food, gave some to Vera Eunice, ate and laid down. When I awoke the rays of the sun were coming through the gaps of the shack.

July 18   I got up at 7. Happy and content. Weariness would be here soon enough. I went to the junk dealer and received 60 cruzeiros. I passed by Arnaldo, bought bread, milk, paid what I owed him, and still had enough to buy Vera some chocolate. I returned to a Hell. I opened the door and threw the children outside. Dona Rosa, as soon as she saw my boy José Carlos, started to fight with him. She didn't want the boy to come near her shack. She ran out with a stick to hit him. A woman of 48 years fighting with a child! At times, after I leave, she comes to my window and throws a filled chamber pot onto the children. When I return I find the pillows dirty and the children fetid. She hates me. She says that the handsome and distinguished men prefer me and that I make more money than she does.

Dona Cecilia appeared. She came to punish my children. I threw a right at her and she stepped back. I told her:

"There are women that say they know how to raise children, but some have children in jails listed as delinquents."

---

[2] Carlos Lacerda: a young energetic politician (current Governor of the State of Guanabara where Rio de Janeiro is located) who is always in the limelight with fiery speeches and ideas for social reform. A newsman as well, he wrote editorials which contributed to the downfall and eventual suicide of Brazil's President Getulio Vargas in 1954. Vargas was a dictator until 1945 and loved by the lower classes. His friends attempted to assassinate Lacerda but killed an army major instead.

She went away. Then came that bitch Angel Mary. I said: "I was fighting with the banknotes, now the small change is arriving. I don't go to anybody's door, and you people who come to my door only bore me. I never bother anyone's children or come to your shack shouting against your kids. And don't think that yours are saints; it's just that I tolerate them."

Dona Silvia came to complain about my children. That they were badly educated. I don't look for defects in children. Neither in mine nor in others. I know that a child is not born with sense. When I speak with a child I use pleasant words. What infuriates me is that the parents come to my door to disrupt my rare moments of inner tranquillity. But when they upset me, I write. I know how to dominate my impulses. I only had two years of schooling, but I got enough to form my character. The only thing that does not exist in the favela is friendship.

Then came the fishmonger Senhor Antonio Lira and he gave me some fish. I started preparing lunch. The women went away, leaving me in peace for today. They had put on their show. My door is actually a theater. All children throw stones, but my boys are the scapegoats. They gossip that I'm not married, but I'm happier than they are. They have husbands but they are forced to beg. They are supported by charity organizations.

My kids are not kept alive by the church's bread. I take on all kinds of work to keep them. And those women have to beg or even steal. At night when they are begging I peacefully sit in my shack listening to Viennese waltzes. While their husbands break the boards of the shack, I and my children sleep peacefully. I don't envy the married women of the favelas who lead lives like Indian slaves.

I never got married and I'm not unhappy. Those who wanted to marry me were mean and the conditions they imposed on me were horrible.

Take Maria José, better known as Zefa, who lives in shack number nine on "B" Street. She is an alcoholic and when she is pregnant she drinks to excess. The children are born and they die before they reach two months. She hates me because my children thrive and I have a radio. One day she asked to borrow my radio. I told her I wouldn't loan it, and as she didn't have any children, she could work and buy one. But it is well known that people who are given to the vice of drink never buy anything. Not even clothes. Drunks don't prosper. Sometimes she throws water on my children. She claims I never punish my kids. I'm not given to violence. José Carlos said:

"Don't be sad, Mama. Our Lady of Aparecida [3] will help you, and when I grow up I'll buy a brick house for you."

I went to collect paper and stayed away from the house an hour. When I returned I saw several people at the river bank. There was a man unconscious from alcohol and the worthless men of the favela were cleaning out his pockets. They stole his money and tore up his documents. It is 5 p.m. Now Senhor Heitor turns on the light. And I, I have to wash the children so they can go to bed, for I have to go out. I need money to pay the light bill. That's the way it is here. Person doesn't use the lights but must pay for them. I left and went to collect paper. I walked fast because it was late. I met a woman complaining about her married life. I listened but said nothing. I tied up the sacks, put the tin cans that I found in another sack, and went home. When I arrived I turned on the radio to see what time it was. It was 11:55. I heated some food, read, undressed, and laid down. Sleep came soon.

July 19 My children talking woke me up at 7 a.m. I got out of bed and went to look for water. The women were already at the spigot. Their cans in a row. When I got there Florentina asked me:

"What political party put up that poster?"

I read P.S.B. and answered Brazilian Socialist Party. Senhor Germano went by and she asked him.

"Senhor Germano, what party is that sign?"

"Janio's!" [4]

She was overjoyed and started to say that Adhemar de Barros [5] was a crook. That only useless people liked and

---

[3] Our Lady of Aparecida: a carved image of the Virgin Mary that legend says appeared in a grotto, and has become the patron saint of Brazil.

[4] Janio Quadros: politician from São Paulo who moved fast from city councilman to President of the Republic. His sudden resignation as Chief Executive in August 1961 touched off a crisis that almost plunged Brazil into a civil war.

[5] Adhemar de Barros: wealthy politician who as mayor then Governor of São Paulo city and State managed to get the support of the lower classes with social projects and promises. He was defeated for President by Janio Quadros in 1960.

respected Dr. Adhemar. I, and Dona Maria Puerta, a very good Spanish woman, defended Adhemar. Dona Maria said:

"I always was an Adhemar supporter. I like him and his wife Dona Leonor very much."

Florentina asked:

"Has he ever given you anything?"

"Yes. He gave us the Clinical Hospital."

My turn came and I put my can under the spigot to fill. Florentina continued praising Janio. The water in the spigot began to diminish. They blamed Rosa. Because she had been carrying water since 4 a.m. and washed all her clothes at home. She must pay 20 cruzeiros a month. My can filled, I went away.

I've been thinking of the problems I've had these days. I can take the ups and downs of life. If I can't store up courage to live, I've resolved to store up patience.

I've never hurt anybody. I'm smarter than that. I don't want any lawsuits. My identification card number is 845.936.

I went to the junk dealer to sell the paper. 55 cruzeiros. I hurried back, bought milk and bread. I made a chocolate drink for the children, made the beds, put beans on the stove, and swept the shack. I called Senhor Ireno Venancio da Silva to make a teeter-totter for the boys. To see if they would stay in the yard so the neighbors won't fight with them. I paid him 16 cruzeiros. While he was making the teeter-totter I went to soap the clothes. When I returned Senhor Ireno was finishing it, and a few more touches and he was done. The children liked the board when it was ready. Everybody wanted to ride at the same time.

I locked the door and went to sell some tin cans. I took the children with me. The day is hot and I like them to get the rays of the sun. What an ordeal! I carried Vera and put the sack on my head. I sold the cans and the scrap. I got 31 cruzeiros. I was happy. I asked:

"Senhor Manuel, didn't you make a mistake?"

"No, why?"

"Because the sack didn't weigh as much as 31 cruzeiros' worth. This amount is just what I need to pay the light bill."

I said good-by and returned home. I made lunch. While the pots boiled, I wrote a little. I gave the children their lunch and went to Klabin paper mill to look for paper. I left the children playing in the yard. I got a lot of paper. I worked fast, thinking that those human beasts are capable of invading my shack and mistreating my children. I worked on, nervous and upset. My head began to ache. They wait for me to leave so they can come to my shack and hurt my children. Always when I'm not at home. When the children are alone they can't defend themselves.

In the favelas children of 15 stay out as late as they want. They mess around with prostitutes and listen to their adventures. There are those who work and those who just drift. The older people work. It's the younger ones who refuse to work. They have their mothers who pick up fruits and vegetables that fall from the street markets.[6] They have the churches who give them bread. They have San Francisco church that once a month gives away necessities like coffee and soap.

They go to the fish market, pick up fish heads, anything they can find. They eat anything. They must have stomachs of reinforced concrete. Sometimes I turn on the radio and dance with the children; we pretend we're boxing. Today I bought candy for them. I gave each one a piece and felt them looking at me a bit differently. My João said:

"What a good mother!"

When those female witches invade my shack, my children throw stones at them. The women scream:

"What uneducated brats!"

I reply:

"My children are defending me. You are ignorant and can't understand that. I'm going to write a book about the favela, and I'm going to tell everything that happened here. And everything that you do to me. I want to write a book, and you with these disgusting scenes are furnishing me with material."

Silvia asked me to take her name out of my book. She said:

"You are a tramp too. You slept in the flophouse. When you end up, you'll be crazy!"

I replied:

"That's true. Those who sleep in the flophouse are the poor. They have nowhere else to turn to, and one place is as good as another. But you, who say you never sleep in the flophouse, what are you doing here in a shack? You were

---

[6] Street markets: portable open-air vegetable and meat stalls that are moved from street to street to accommodate a large population where supermarkets are virtually unknown. Vendors are mostly Portuguese immigrants selling everything from shoes to ladies' underwear.

born to live in a fine house. How come your life turned out like mine?"

She said:

"The only thing you know how to do is pick up paper."

I said:

"I pick up paper. I'm proving that I'm alive, at least."

I am living in a favela. But if God helps me, I'll get out of here. I hope the politicians tear down the favelas. There are people who take advantage of the way they live to bully those weaker than themselves. There is a house here that has five children and an old woman who walks the entire day begging. There are wives that when their husbands are ill go out and support the family. The husbands, when they see their wives taking care of the home, never get well again.

Today I didn't go out looking for paper. I'm going to lie down. I'm not tired or sleepy. Yesterday I drank a beer and today I want another. But I'm not going to drink. I don't want that curse. I have responsibilities. My children! And the money that I spend on beer takes away from the essentials we need. What I can't stand in the favelas are the fathers who send their children out to buy *pigna* [7] and then give some to the children to drink.

They laugh:

"He's got worms. He's gotta drink it. Doctor's orders!"

My children can't stand alcohol. My son João said:

"Mama, when I grow up I'm not going to drink. A man who drinks doesn't buy clothes, doesn't have a radio, and doesn't build himself a brick house."

Today was a blessed day for me. The troublemakers of the favela see that I'm writing and know that it's about them. They decided to leave me in peace. In the favelas the men are more tolerant, more understanding. The rowdies are the women. Their intrigues are like Carlos Lacerda's and grate against the nerves. My nerves can't stand it. But I'm strong. I don't let anything bother me deeply. I don't get discouraged.

July 20 I got out of bed at 4 a.m. to write. I opened the door and gazed at the starry sky. When the sun started to climb I went for water. I was lucky! The women weren't at the spigot. I filled my cans and hurried off. I went to Arnaldo to get bread and milk. When I was returning I met Ismael

---

[7] *Pinga:* a white fiery liquor made from sugar cane. Powerful and potent, it is the favorite drink of Brazil's poor, who can get drunk on it for less than ten cents a bottle.

with a knife at least a foot long. He told me he was waiting for Binidito and Miguel to kill them, for they had beaten him up while he was drunk.

I advised him not to fight, because crime doesn't work to anyone's advantage and only disrupts life. Then I smelled the alcohol and stopped. I know that drunks don't pay attention. Ismael, when he's not boozed up, shows his intelligence. He used to be a telegraph operator and a member of the Esoteric Circle Church. He can quote from the Bible and likes to give advice. But now he's not worth anything. He lets alcohol control him, but even so at times his advice is good for those who want to lead a decent life.

I prepared breakfast. Every child wants something different. Vera: oatmeal. João: black coffee. José Carlos: milk. And I: cream of wheat.

At this moment I can't give my children a decent house to live in, so I try to give them decent food.

They finished breakfast and I wished the dishes. Then I went to wash clothes. I don't have a man at home. There is just me and my children, so I can't relax. My dream is to be very clean, to wear expensive clothes and live in a comfortable house, but it's not possible. I am not unhappy with the work I do. I am used to being dirty. I've carried paper for eight years. What disgusts me is that I must live in a favela.

During the day the youths of 15 to 18 sit on the ground and talk of robbery. They just tried to hold up Senhor Raymundo Guello's store. One of them was wounded by a bullet and scattered the loot as he fell. The robbery took place at 4 a.m. When the dawn came children looked for the money in the street and a vacant lot. There was a child who found 20 cruzeiros. He showed the money around the favela and smiled. But the judge was severe, punishing without pity.

I went to the river to wash clothes and met Dona Mariana. She is a pleasant and decent woman with nine children and a nice home. She and her husband have given them an education. She tells them to live in peace and to raise children. She was also going to wash clothes. She told me that Dona Geralda's Binidito was locked up all day. The radio patrol is tired of coming to look for him. They found him some work to do at the police station. I thought that was very funny and I laughed. Meanwhile I spread the clothes on the grass and went to look for paper. What an ordeal it is to search for paper. I have to carry my daughter Vera Eunice. She is only two years old and doesn't like to stay at home. I put the sack on my head and carried her in my arms. I bore the weight of the sack on my head and the weight of Vera Eunice in my arms. Sometimes it makes me angry. Then I get ahold of myself. She's not guilty because she's in the world.

I reflected: I've got to be tolerant with my children. They don't have anyone in the world but me. How sad is the condition of a woman alone without a man at home.

Here all the women pick on me. They say that I talk too well and that I know how to attract men. When I'm nervous I don't like to argue. I prefer to write. Every day I write. I sit in the yard and write.

I can't go looking for paper. Vera Eunice doesn't want to sleep and neither does José Carlos. Silvia and her husband are quarreling. They've got nine children but don't respect them. Every day they fight.

I sold the paper and got 140 cruzeiros. I worked too hard and felt ill. I took some Dr. Ross's "Pills of Life" for my liver and lay down. When I was sleeping I was awakened by the voice of Antonio Andrade arguing with his wife.

July 21   I woke with the voice of Dona Maria asking me if I wanted to buy any bananas or lettuce. I glanced at the children. They were still sleeping. I didn't answer. When they see fruit I have to buy it. I sent my boy João to Arnaldo's to buy sugar and bread. Then I went to wash clothes. While the clothes were bleaching I sat on the sidewalk and wrote. A man passed by and asked me:

"What are you writing?"

"All the cheating that the favela dwellers practice. Those human wrecks."

He said:

"Write it and give it to an editor so he can make revisions."

He looked at the children around me and asked:

"These kids are yours?"

I looked at the children. Of mine, there were only two. But as they were all the same color, I told him yes.

"Where does your husband work?"

"I don't have a husband and I don't want one!"

A white woman who was listening hurried away. I thought: maybe she didn't appreciate my answer.

"That's a lot of children to take care of."

He opened his billfold. I thought: now he's going to give money to one of those kids thinking that all of them are mine. That was a stupid lie!

But Vera Eunice grabbed his arm and said:

"Give. Me. Shoes."

I said:

"She's saying that she wants the money to buy shoes."

He said:

"Give this to your mother."

I raised my eyes and looked at him. Two little girls with him called him "Daddy." I've seen him. Once I talked with him in a drugstore when I took Vera to get a flu shot. He walked on. I looked at the money he gave Vera. A hundred cruzeiros!

In a few minutes the story spread that Vera had gotten a hundred cruzeiros. I thought of the efficiency of the human tongue to transmit news. The children crowded around. I got up and went to sit near Dona Mariana's house. I asked her for a little coffee. I'm used to drinking coffee in Senhor Lino's house. Everything I ask them to loan me, they loan me. When I go to pay them, they never take it.

Afterward I went to wring out the clothes and returned to make lunch. Today I'm singing. I'm happy and I've asked the neighbors not to bother me. All of us have one happy day—today is mine!

A girl by the name of Amalia said that a spirit had possessed her mother. She was running around trying to throw herself into the river. Many women tried to stop her. I spent the rest of the afternoon writing. At 4:30 Senhor Heitor turned on the lights. I gave the children a bath and got ready to go out. I went out to pick up paper but I felt ill. I hurried because it was cold. When I got home it was 10:30. I turned on the radio, took a bath, and heated some food. I read a little. I don't know how to sleep without reading. I like to leaf through a book. The book is man's best invention so far.

July 22   There are times when I am fed up with the worrisome life I lead. And there are times when I conform to it. I talked to a woman who was raising a little colored girl. She is so good to the child. She buys her expensive dresses. I said:

"In the old days it was the blacks who took care of the

whites. Today it is the whites who are taking care of the blacks."

The woman told me she had raised the child since it was nine months old, and that the little girl sleeps with her and calls her "Mother."

A boy came by. She said it was her boy. I told a few jokes. They laughed and I went on my way singing.

I started to collect paper. I went up Tiradentes Street, paying my respects to the women I knew. The dry cleaner's wife said:

"Poor thing. She is so good."

I kept on repeating in my mind: "She is so good."

I like to stay inside the house with the door locked. I don't like to stay on street corners talking. I like to be alone and read. Or write! I turned up Frei Antonio Galvão Street. Almost no paper. Dona Nair Barros was at her window. I told her that I lived in a favela. And that the favela is the worst slum that exists.

I filled two sacks on Alfredo Maia Street. I took one to the junk yard and returned for the other. I traveled on other streets and conversed a little with Senhor João Pedro. I went to a colored woman's house to take her some cans that she had asked for. Big cans for planting flowers. I stayed there, getting to know this very clean Negress who spoke so well. She said that she was a seamstress but didn't like her profession, and that she admired me. I looked for paper and sang.

I am very happy. I sing every morning. I'm like the birds who sing only in the morning because in the morning I'm always happy. The first thing that I do is open the window and think about heaven.

July 23 I turned on the radio to listen to a play. I fixed lunch and laid down. I slept an hour and a half. I never heard the end of the drama. I started to write my diary. Every now and then I stopped to scold my children. There was a knocking at the door. I told João to open it and ask them to enter. It was Senhor João. He asked me where he could find potato leaves to make a mouth wash for his daughter. I said that at the Portuguese lady it was possible to find them. He wanted to know what I was writing. I replied it was my diary.

"I never saw a black who liked books as much as you do!"

Everyone has an ideal in life. Mine is to be able to read.

Senhor João gave 50 centavos to each child. When he first met me I only had two children.

Nobody came to upset me. Thank God.

July 24 I got up at 5 o'clock to carry water. Today is Sunday and the women go later for water. But now I'm in the habit of getting up early. I bought bread and soap. I put beans on the stove and went to wash clothes. At the river Adair Mathias was complaining that her mother had gone away and she had to fix lunch and wash clothes. She said that her mother was well, but that someone had put a curse on her. The voodoo priest said it was a witch. But the curse that has invaded the Mathias family is alcohol. That's my opinion.

Dona Mariana complained that her husband was taking his time about returning home. I put the clothes in the sun to bleach and went to make lunch. When I got home I found Dona Francisca fighting with my son João.

A woman of 40 years arguing with a child of eight! I put the boy inside and locked the door. She continued shouting. To make her stop I had to shout:

"Shut your tubercular mouth!"

I don't like to mention physical ills because it's nobody's fault if they have a contagious disease. But when a person gets so that they can't stand the ravings of an illiterate, they have to shout their illnesses.

Senhor João came looking for potato leaves. I told him:

"Oh, if I could move out of this favela! I feel like I'm in hell!"

I sat in the sun to write. Silvia's daughter, a girl of six, passed by and said:

"You're writing again, stinking nigger!"

Her mother heard and didn't say anything. It's the mothers that put them up to it.

July 25 I got up happy. I'm singing. The only peaceful hours I have here in the favela are in the morning.

Today Dona Francisca sent her six-year-old daughter to provoke me, but I was very sleepy. I shut the door and lay down. I went to see the newborn son of Dona Maria Puerta, a Spaniard of the first class. The jewel of the favela. Gold in the midst of lead.

July 27 I got up in the morning and went to look for water. I had to argue with Silvia's husband because he didn't want to let me fill my cans. I didn't have any money in the house. I heated some breakfast food and fed the children.

Senhor Ireno told me that last night there was a robbery in the favela. That someone stole clothes from Dona Florela and 1,000 cruzeiros from Dona Paulina. My shack is also being visited. For two nights now I've not gone looking for paper. To stop worrying I took the radio to Dona Florela's house. And I'm the one who wants to buy a sewing machine —just one more thing to worry about!

Senhor Gino came to ask me to go to his shack. That I am neglecting him. I answered: no!

I am writing a book to sell. I am hoping that with this money I can buy a place and leave the favela. I don't have time to go to anybody's house. Senhor Gino insisted. He told me:

"Just knock and I'll open the door."

But my heart didn't ask me to go to his room.

July 28 I was horrified! Someone burned five sacks of my paper. Dona Elvira's granddaughter, who has two girls and doesn't want any more children because her husband earns very little, said:

"We saw the smoke. And besides you put the sacks there in the street. Hide them where no one can see them." *Favelados* live by robbing from one another.

I think it was she who burnt my bags. They made me sick so I went away. Someone told me that they are crooked Portuguese and that Dona Elvira never does anyone a favor. Now I've been warned. I don't resent it. I'm so used to human malice.

I know I'll need those sacks badly.

(End of diary for 1955)

The DIARY of
CAROLINA MARIA DE JESUS

1958

May 2, 1958 I'm not lazy. There are times when I try to keep up my diary. But then I think it's not worth it and figure I'm wasting my time.

I've made a promise to myself. I want to treat people that I know with more consideration. I want to have a pleasant smile for children and the employed.

I received a summons to appear at 8 p.m. at police station number 12. I spent the day looking for paper. At night my feet pained me so I couldn't walk. It started to rain. I went to the station and took José Carlos with me. The summons was for him. José Carlos is nine years old.

May 3 I went to the market at Carlos de Campos Street looking for any old thing. I got a lot of greens. But it didn't help much, for I've got no cooking fat. The children are upset because there's nothing to eat.

May 6 In the morning I went for water. I made João carry it. I was happy, then I received another summons. I was inspired yesterday and my verses were so pretty, I forgot to go to the station. It was 11:00 when I remembered the invitation from the illustrious lieutenant of the 12th precinct.

My advice to would-be politicians is that people do not tolerate hunger. It's necessary to know hunger to know how to describe it.

They are putting up a circus here at Araguaia Street. The Nilo Circus Theater.

May 9 I looked for paper but I didn't like it. Then I thought: I'll pretend that I'm dreaming.

May 10 I went to the police station and talked to the lieutenant. What a pleasant man! If I had known he was going to be so pleasant, I'd have gone on the first summons. The lieutenant was interested in my boys' education. He said the favelas have an unhealthy atmosphere where the people have more chance to go wrong than to become useful to state and country. I thought: if he knows this why doesn't he make a report and send it to the politicians? To Janio Quadros, Kubitschek,[8] and Dr. Adhemar de Barros? Now he tells me this, I a poor garbage collector. I can't even solve my own problems.

Brazil needs to be led by a person who has known hunger. Hunger is also a teacher.

Who has gone hungry learns to think of the future and of the children.

May 11 Today is Mother's Day. The sky is blue and white. It seems that even nature wants to pay homage to the mothers who feel unhappy because they can't realize the desires of their children.

The sun keeps climbing. Today it's not going to rain. Today is our day.

Dona Teresinha came to visit me. She gave me 15 cruzeiros and said it was for Vera to go to the circus. But I'm going to use the money to buy bread tomorrow because I only have four cruzeiros.

Yesterday I got half a pig's head at the slaughterhouse. We ate the meat and saved the bones. Today I put the bones on to boil and into the broth I put some potatoes. My children are always hungry. When they are starving they aren't so fussy about what they eat.

Night came. The stars are hidden. The shack is filled with mosquitoes. I lit a page from a newspaper and ran it over the walls. This is the way the favela dwellers kill mosquitoes.

May 13 At dawn it was raining. Today is a nice day for me, it's the anniversary of the Abolition. The day we celebrate the freeing of the slaves. In the jails the Negroes were the scapegoats. But now the whites are more educated and don't treat us any more with contempt. May God enlighten the whites so that the Negroes may have a happier life.

It continued to rain and I only have beans and salt.

---

[8] Juscelino Kubitschek: President of Brazil from 1956 to 1961.

The rain is strong but even so I sent the boys to school. I'm writing until the rain goes away so I can go to Senhor Manuel and sell scrap. With that money I'm going to buy rice and sausage. The rain has stopped for a while. I'm going out.

I feel so sorry for my children. When they see the things to eat that I come home with they shout:

"Viva Mama!"

Their outbursts please me. But I've lost the habit of smiling. Ten minutes later they want more food. I sent João to ask Dona Ida for a little pork fat. She didn't have any. I sent her a note:

"Dona Ida, I beg you to help me get a little pork fat, so I can make soup for the children. Today it's raining and I can't go looking for paper. Thank you, Carolina."

It rained and got colder. Winter had arrived and in winter people eat more. Vera asked for food, and I didn't have any. It was the same old show. I had two cruzeiros and wanted to buy a little flour to make a *virado*.[9] I went to ask Dona Alice for a little pork. She gave me pork and rice. It was 9 at night when we ate.

And that is the way on May 13, 1958 I fought against the real slavery—hunger!

May 15 On the nights they have a party they don't let anybody sleep. The neighbors in the brick houses near by have signed a petition to get rid of the *favelados*. But they won't get their way. The neighbors in the brick houses say:

"The politicians protect the *favelados*."

Who protects us are the public and the Order of St. Vincent Church. The politicians only show up here during election campaigns. Senhor Candido Sampaio, when he was city councilman in 1953, spent his Sundays here in the favela. He was so nice. He drank our coffee, drinking right out of our cups. He made us laugh with his jokes. He played with our children. He left a good impression here and when he was candidate for state deputy, he won. But the Chamber of Deputies didn't do one thing for the *favelados*. He doesn't visit us any more.

I classify São Paulo this way: The Governor's Palace is the living room. The mayor's office is the dining room

---

[9] *Virado:* a dish of black beans, manioc flour, pork, and eggs.

and the city is the garden. And the favela is the back yard
where they throw the garbage.

The night is warm. The sky is peppered with stars. I
have the crazy desire to cut a piece of the sky to make a
dress. I hear some yelling and go into the street. It is
Ramiro who wants to give it to Senhor Binidito. A mis-
understanding. A tile fell on the electric line and turned
off the lights in Ramiro's house. For this Ramiro wants to
beat Senhor Binidito. Because Ramiro is strong and Binidito
is weak.

Ramiro got angry because I was on Binidito's side. I
tried to fix the wires. While I was trying to repair them
Ramiro wanted to hit Binidito but was so drunk he couldn't
even stand up. I can't describe the effects of alcohol because I don't drink. I drank once, just to try it, but the
alcohol made me silly.

While I was working to repair the light, Ramiro said:
"Turn on the light! Turn on the light or I'll smash your
face."

The wire wasn't long enough to connect. It needed to be
mended. I'm not an expert in electrical matters. I sent for
Senhor Alfredo, who is professionally an electrician. He was
nervous and kept glancing at Binidito. Juana, who is the
wife of Binidito, gave 50 cruzeiros to Senhor Alfredo. He
took the money, didn't smile, but was pleased. I could tell
by his face. In the end money always dissipates nervousness.
May 16 I awoke upset. I wanted to stay at home but
didn't have anything to eat.

I'm not going to eat because there is very little bread.
I wonder if I'm the only one who leads this kind of life.
What can I hope for the future? I wonder if the poor of
other countries suffer like the poor of Brazil. I was so
unhappy that I started to fight without reason with my boy
José Carlos.

A truck came to the favela. The driver and his helper
threw away some cans. It was canned sausage. I thought:
this is what these hardhearted businessmen do. They stay
waiting for the prices to go up so they can earn more. And
when it rots they throw it to the buzzards and the unhappy
favelados.

There wasn't any fighting. Even I found it dull. I watched
the children open the cans of sausages and exclaim:
"Ummm! Delicious!"

Dona Alice gave me one to try, but the can was bulging. It was rotten.

May 18 In the favela everything spreads in a minute. The news has gone around that Dona Maria José is dead. Various persons came to see her. The St. Vincent brother who took care of her showed up. He had come to visit her every Sunday. He is not disgusted by the *favelados* and treats their miseries with tenderness. There's no comparison with that so-called State Social Service.

The coffin arrived. It was purple. The color of the bitterness that encloses the hearts of the *favelados*.

Dona Maria was a Believer and said that the Believers before dying were already in Heaven. The burial is at 3 this afternoon. The Believers are singing a hymn. Their voices are sweet. I have the feeling that it's the angels who are singing. I don't see one drunk. Maybe out of respect for the dead, but I doubt it. I think it's because they don't have the money.

The coach arrived to deliver the lifeless body of Dona Maria José to her true home—the tomb. Dona Maria José was very good. They say that the living must forgive the dead, and that all of us have our moments of weakness. The funeral car arrived and is waiting for the hour to leave for the burial.

I'm going to stop writing. I'm going to wring the clothes I left soaking yesterday. I don't like to see burials.

May 19 I left the bed at 5 a.m. The sparrows have just begun their morning symphony. The birds must be happier than we are. Perhaps happiness and equality reigns among them. The world of the birds must be better than that of the *favelados,* who lie down but don't sleep because they go to bed hungry.

What our President Senhor Juscelino has in his favor is his voice. He sings like a bird and his voice is pleasant to the ears. And now the bird is living in a golden cage called Catete Palace. Be careful, little bird, that you don't lose this cage, because cats when they are hungry think of birds in cages. The *favelados* are the cats, and they are hungry.

I broke my train of thought when I heard the voice of the baker:

"Here you go! Fresh bread, and right on time for breakfast!"

How little he knows that in the favela there are only a

few who have breakfast. The *favelados* eat only when they have something to eat. All the families who live in the favela have children. A Spanish woman lives here named Dona Maria Puerta. She bought some land and started to economize so she could build a house. When she finished construction her children were weak with pneumonia. And there are eight children.

There have been people who visited us and said:

"Only pigs could live in a place like this. This is the pigsty of São Paulo."

I'm starting to lose my interest in life. It's beginning to revolt me and my revulsion is just.

I washed the floor because I'm expecting a visit from a future deputy and he wants me to make some speeches for him. He says he wants to know the favelas and if he is elected he's going to abolish them.

The sky was the color of indigo, and I understood that I adore my Brazil. My glance went over to the trees that are planted at the beginning of Pedro Vicente Street. The leaves moved by themselves. I thought: they are applauding my gesture of love to my country. I went on looking for paper. Vera was smiling and I thought of Casemiro de Abreu, the Brazilian poet who said: "Laugh, child. Life is beautiful." Life was good in that era. Because now in this era it's necessary to say: "Cry, child. Life is bitter."

I went on so preoccupied that I didn't even notice the gardens of the city. It's the season for white flowers, the predominating color. And in the month of May the altars must be adorned with white flowers. We must thank God or Nature, who gave us the stars that adorn the sky, for the flowers that adorn the parks and the fields and the forests.

When I was going up Southern Cross Avenue I saw a woman with blue shoes and a blue handbag. Vera told me:

"Look, Mama, what a beautiful woman. She is going in my car."

My daughter Vera Eunice says she is going to buy a car and will only drive beautiful people in it. The woman smiled and Vera went on:

"You smell so good!"

I saw that my daughter knew how to flatter. The woman opened her bag and gave me 20 cruzeiros.

Here in the favela almost everyone has a difficult fight to live. But I am the only one who writes of what suffering

is. I do this for the good of the others. Many look in the
garbage for shoes to wear. But the shoes are weak and only
last six days. In the old days, that is from 1950–1958, the
favelados sang. They had parties. 1957, 1958 life was getting
tougher and tougher. Now there isn't even money for them
to buy *pinga*. The parties were shortened until they snuffed
themselves out. The other day I met a policeman. He asked
me:

"You still live in the favela?"

"Why?"

"Because your family has left the Radio Patrol in peace."

"There's no money left over to buy booze!" I snapped.

I put João and Vera to bed and went looking for José
Carlos. I telephoned the Central Police Station. The phone
doesn't always resolve things. I took a street car and went
there. I didn't feel cold. I felt as if my blood was 40 degrees.
I spoke with the Female Police who told me that José Carlos
was at Asdrubal Nascimento Street (juvenile court). What a
relief! Only a mother could appreciate it.

I went toward Asdrubal Nascimento. I don't know how to
walk at night. The glare of the lights turns me around. I
have to keep asking. I like the night only to contemplate
the shining stars, to read and to write. During the night it
is quieter.

I arrived at Asdrubal Nascimento and the guard told me
to wait. I looked at the children. Some were crying but others
were furious with the interference of a law that didn't permit them to do as they pleased. José Carlos was crying.
When he heard my voice he became happy. I could feel his
contentment. He looked at me and it was the tenderest look
I have ever received in my life.

At 8:30 that night I was in the favela breathing the smell
of excrement mixed with the rotten earth. When I am in
the city I have the impression that I am in a living room
with crystal chandeliers, rugs of velvet, and satin cushions.
And when I'm in the favela I have the impression that I'm a
useless object, destined to be forever in a garbage dump.

May 20 Day was breaking when I got out of bed. Vera
woke up and sang and asked me to sing with her. We sang.
Then José Carlos and João joined in.

The morning was damp and foggy. The sun was rising
but its heat didn't chase away the cold. I stayed thinking:
there are seasons when the sun dominates. There's a season

for the rain. There's a season for the wind. Now is the time for the cold. Among them there are no rivalries. Each one has a time.

I opened the window and watched the women passing by with their coats discolored and worn by time. It won't be long until these coats which they got from others, and which should be in a museum, will be replaced by others. The politicians must give us things. That includes me too, because I'm also a *favelado*. I'm one of the discarded. I'm in the garbage dump and those in the garbage dump either burn themselves or throw themselves into ruin.

The women that I see passing are going to church begging for bread for their children. Brother Luiz gives it to them while their husbands remain home under the blankets. Some because they can't find jobs. Others because they are sick. Others because they are drunk.

I don't bother myself about their men. If they give a ball and I don't show up, it's because I don't like to dance. I only get involved in fights when I think I can prevent a crime. I don't know what started this unfriendliness of mine. I have a hard cold look for both men and women. My smile and my soft smooth words I save for children.

There is a teen-ager named Julião who beats his father at times. When he hits his father it is with such sadism and pleasure. He thinks he is unconquerable. He beats the old man as if he were beating a drum. The father wants him to study law. When Julião was arrested the father went with him with his eyes filled with tears. As if he was accompanying a saint in a procession. Julião is a rebel, but without a cause. They don't need to live in a favela; they have a home on Villa Maria hill.

Sometimes families move into the favela with children. In the beginning they are educated, friendly. Days later they use foul language, are mean and quarrelsome. They are diamonds turned to lead. They are transformed from objects that were in the living room to objects banished to the garbage dump.

For me the world instead of evolving is turning primitive. Those who don't know hunger will say: "Whoever wrote this is crazy." But who has gone hungry can say:

"Well, Dona Carolina. The basic necessities must be within reach of everyone."

How horrible it is to see a child eat and ask: "Is there

more?" This word "more" keeps ringing in the mother's head as she looks in the pot and doesn't have any more.

When a politician tells us in his speeches that he is on the side of the people, that he is only in politics in order to improve our living conditions, asking for our votes, promising to freeze prices, he is well aware that by touching on these grave problems he will win at the polls. Afterward he divorces himself from the people. He looks at them with half-closed eyes, and with a pride that hurts us.

When I arrived from the Palace that is the city, my children ran to tell me that they had found some macaroni in the garbage. As the food supply was low I cooked some of the macaroni with beans. And my son João said to me:

"Uh, huh. You told me we weren't going to eat any more things from the garbage."

It was the first time I had failed to keep my word. I said "I had faith in President Kubitschek."

"You had faith, and now you don't have it any more?"

"No, my son, democracy is losing its followers. In our country everything is weakening. The money is weak. Democracy is weak and the politicians are very weak. Everything that is weak dies one day."

The politicians know that I am a poetess. And that a poet will even face death when he sees his people oppressed.

May 21 I spent a horrible night. I dreamt I lived in a decent house that had a bathroom, kitchen, pantry, and even a maid's room. I was going to celebrate the birthday of my daughter Vera Eunice. I went and bought some small pots that I had wanted for a long time. Because I was able to buy. I sat at the table to eat. The tablecloth was white as a lily. I ate a steak, bread and butter, fried potatoes, and a salad. When I reached for another steak I woke up. What bitter reality! I don't live in the city. I live in the favela. In the mud on the banks of the Tieté River. And with only nine cruzeiros. I don't even have sugar, because yesterday after I went out the children ate what little I had.

Who must be a leader is he who has the ability. He who has pity and friendship for the people. Those who govern our country are those who have money, who don't know what hunger is, or pain or poverty. If the majority revolt, what can the minority do? I am on the side of the poor, who are an arm. An undernourished arm. We must free the country of the profiteering politicians.

Yesterday I ate that macaroni from the garbage with fear of death, because in 1953 I sold scrap over there in Zinho. There was a pretty little black boy. He also went to sell scrap in Zinho. He was young and said that those who should look for paper were the old. One day I was collecting scrap when I stopped at Bom Jardim Avenue. Someone had thrown meat into the garbage, and he was picking out the pieces. He told me:

"Take some, Carolina. It's still fit to eat."

He gave me some, and so as not to hurt his feelings, I accepted. I tried to convince him not to eat that meat, or the hard bread gnawed by the rats. He told me no, because it was two days since he had eaten. He made a fire and roasted the meat. His hunger was so great that he couldn't wait for the meat to cook. He heated it and ate. So as not to remember that scene, I left thinking: I'm going to pretend I wasn't there. This can't be real in a rich country like mine. I was disgusted with that Social Service that had been created to readjust the maladjusted, but took no notice of we marginal people. I sold the scrap at Zinho and returned to São Paulo's back yard, the favela.

The next day I found that little black boy dead. His toes were spread apart. The space must have been eight inches between them. He had blown up as if made out of rubber. His toes looked like a fan. He had no documents. He was buried like any other "Joe." Nobody tried to find out his name. The marginal people don't have names.

Once every four years the politicians change without solving the problem of hunger that has its headquarters in the favela and its branch offices in the workers' homes.

When I went to get water I saw a poor woman collapse near the pump because last night she slept without dinner. She was undernourished. The doctors that we have in politics know this.

Now I'm going to Dona Julita's house to work for her. I went looking for paper. Senhor Samuel weighed it. I got 12 cruzeiros. I went up Tiradentes Avenue looking for paper. I came to Brother Antonio Santana de Galvão Street, number 17, to work for Dona Julita. She told me not to fool with men because I might have another baby and that afterward men won't give anything to take care of the child. I smiled and thought: In relations with men, I've had some bitter experiences. Now I'm mature, reached a stage of life where my judgment has grown roots.

I found a sweet potato and a carrot in the garbage. When I got back to the favela my boys were gnawing on a piece of hard bread. I thought: for them to eat this bread, they need electric teeth.

I don't have any lard. I put meat on the fire with some tomatoes that I found at the Peixe canning factory. I put in the carrot and the sweet potato and water. As soon as it was boiling, I put in the macaroni that the boys found in the garbage. The *favelados* are the few who are convinced that in order to live, they must imitate the vultures. I don't see any help from the Social Service regarding the *favelados*. Tomorrow I'm not going to have bread. I'm going to cook a sweet potato.

May 22 Today I'm sad. I'm nervous. I don't know if I should start crying or start running until I fall unconscious. At dawn it was raining. I couldn't go out to get any money. I spent the day writing. I cooked the macaroni and I'll warm it up again for the children. I cooked the potatoes and they ate them. I have a few tin cans and a little scrap that I'm going to sell to Senhor Manuel. When João came home from school I sent him to sell the scrap. He got 13 cruzeiros. He bought a glass of mineral water: two cruzeiros. I was furious with him. Where had he seen a *favelado* with such highborn tastes?

The children eat a lot of bread. They like soft bread but when they don't have it, they eat hard bread.

Hard is the bread that we eat. Hard is the bed on which we sleep. Hard is the life of the *favelado*.

Oh, São Paulo! A queen that vainly shows her skyscrapers that are her crown of gold. All dressed up in velvet and silk but with cheap stockings underneath—the favela.

The money didn't stretch far enough to buy meat, so I cooked macaroni with a carrot. I didn't have any grease, it was horrible. Vera was the only one who complained yet asked for more.

"Mama, sell me to Dona Julita, because she has delicious food."

I know that there exist Brazilians here inside São Paulo who suffer more than I do. In June of '57 I felt rich and passed through the offices of the Social Service. I had carried a lot of scrap iron and got pains in my kidneys. So as not to see my children hungry I asked for help from the famous Social Service. It was there that I saw the tears slipping from the eyes of the poor. How painful it is to see the dramas that are played out there. The coldness in which they treat the poor. The only things they want to know about them is their name and address.

I went to the Governor's Palace.[10] The Palace sent me to an office at Brigadeiro Luis Antonio Avenue. They in turn sent me to the Social Service at the Santa Casa charity hospital. There I talked with Dona Maria Aparecida, who listened to me, said many things yet said nothing. I decided to go back to the Palace. I talked with Senhor Alcides. He is not Japanese yet is as yellow as rotten butter. I said to Senhor Alcides:

"I came here to ask for help because I'm ill. You sent me to Brigadeiro Luis Antonio Avenue, and I went. There they sent me to the Santa Casa. And I spent all the money I have on transportation."

"Take her!"

They wouldn't let me leave. A soldier put his bayonet at my chest. I looked the soldier in the eyes and saw that he had pity on me. I told him:

"I am poor. That's why I came here."

Dr. Osvaldo de Barros entered, a false philanthropist in São Paulo who is masquerading as St. Vincent de Paul. He said:

"Call a squad car!"

The policeman took me back to the favela and warned me that the next time I made a scene at the welfare agency I would be locked up.

Welfare agency! Welfare for whom?

May 23 I got up feeling sad this morning because it was raining. The shack is in terrible disorder. And I don't have soap to wash the dishes. I say "dishes" from force of habit. But they are really tin cans. If I had soap I would wash the clothes. I'm really not negligent. If I walk around dirty it's because I'm trapped in the life of a *favelado*. I've come to the conclusion that for those who aren't going to Heaven, it doesn't help to look up. It's the same with us who don't like the favela, but are obliged to live in one. . . . It doesn't help to look up.

10 Like most Brazilians, Carolina believes in going straight to the top to make her complaints.

I made a meal. The grease frying in the pan was beautiful. What a dazzling display! The children smile watching the food cooking in the pans. Still more when it is rice and beans—it's a holiday for them.

In the old days macaroni was the most expensive dish. Now it's rice and beans that have replaced the macaroni. They've crossed over to the side of the nobility. Even you, rice and beans, have deserted us! You who were the friends of the marginal ones, the *favelados*, the needy. Just look. They are not within reach of the unhappy ones of the Garbage Dump. Who has not flown off is senhor cornmeal. But the children don't like cornmeal.

When I put the food on the table João smiled. He ate and didn't mention the black color of the beans.[11] Because black is our life. Everything is black around us.

In the streets and shops I see the posters with the names of candidates for deputy. Some names are already known. They are the repeaters who have already failed once at the ballot boxes. But the people are not interested in elections. Our elections are just a Trojan Horse that appears once every four years.

The sky is beautiful, worthy of contemplation because the drifting clouds are forming dazzling landscapes. Soft breezes pass by carrying the perfume of flowers. And the sun is always punctual at rising and setting. The birds travel in space, showing off in their happiness. The night brings up the sparkling stars to adorn the blue sky. There are so many beautiful things in the world that are impossible to describe. Only one thing saddens us: the prices when we go shopping. They overshadow all the beauty that exists.

Theresa, Meryi's sister, drank poison. And for no reason. They say she found a note from a woman in her lover's pocket. It ate away her mouth, her throat, and her stomach. She lost a lot of blood. The doctors say that even if she does get well she will be helpless. She has two sons, one four years old and the other nine months.

May 26 At dawn it was raining. I only have four cruzeiros, a little food left over from yesterday, and some bones. I went to look for water to boil the bones. There is still a little

---

[11] Black beans in almost every part of Brazil, except Rio, are looked down upon as the lowest thing that can be eaten. In the northeast poor families shut their windows out of shame that neighbors will see them eating black beans rather than brown ones.

macaroni and I made a soup for the children. I saw a neighbor washing beans.[12] How envious I became. It's been two weeks that I haven't washed clothes because I haven't any soap. I sold some boards for 40 cruzeiros. The woman told me she'd pay today. If she pays I'll buy soap.

For days there hasn't been a policeman in the favela, but today one came because Julião beat his father. He gave him such a violent blow that the old man cried and went to call the police.

May 27   It seems that the slaughterhouse threw kerosene on their garbage dump so the *favelados* would not look for meat to eat. I didn't have any breakfast and walked around half dizzy. The daze of hunger is worse than that of alcohol. The daze of alcohol makes us sing, but the one of hunger makes us shake. I know how horrible it is to only have air in the stomach.

I began to have a bitter taste in my mouth. I thought: is there no end to the bitterness of life? I think that when I was born I was marked by fate to go hungry. I filled one sack of paper. When I entered Paulo Guimarães Street, a woman gave me some newspapers. They were clean and I went to the junk yard picking up everything that I found. Steel, tin, coal, everything serves the *favelado*. Leon weighed the paper and I got six cruzeiros.

I wanted to save the money to buy beans but I couldn't because my stomach was creaming and torturing me.

I decided to do something about it and bought a bread roll. What a surprising effect food has on our organisms. Before I ate, I saw the sky, the trees, and the birds all yellow, but after I ate, everything was normal to my eyes.

Food in the stomach is like fuel in machines. I was able to work better. My body stopped weighing me down. I started to walk faster. I had the feeling that I was gliding in space. I started to smile as if I was witnessing a beautiful play. And will there ever be a drama more beautiful than that of eating? I felt that I was eating for the first time in my life.

The Radio Patrol arrived. They came to take the two Negro boys who had broken into the power station. Four and six years old. It's easy to see that they are of the favela. Favela

---

[12] Beans, like rice, must be picked over to get rid of the rotten kernels, and then washed to take away dust and pieces of dirt and other foreign matter. The *favelados* buy these staples at street fairs from huge wooden bins that are never covered over.

children are the most ragged children in the city. What they can find in the streets they eat. Banana peels, melon rind, and even pineapple husks. Anything that is too tough to chew, they grind. These boys had their pockets filled with aluminum coins, that new money in circulation.

May 28   It dawned raining. I only have three cruzeiros because I loaned Leila five so she could go get her daughter in the hospital. I'm confused and don't know where to begin. I want to write, I want to work, I want to wash clothes. I'm cold and I don't have any shoes to wear. The children's shoes are worn out.

The worst thing in the favela is that there are children here. All the children of the favela know what a woman's body looks like. Because when the couples that are drunk fight, the woman, so as not to get a beating, runs naked into the street. When the fights start the *favelados* leave whatever they are doing to be present at the battle. So that when the woman goes running naked it's a real show for Joe Citizen. Afterward the comments begin among the children:

"Fernanda ran out nude when Armin was hitting her."

"Oh, I didn't see it. Damn!"

"What does a naked woman look like?"

And then the other, in order to tell him, puts his mouth near his ear. And the loud laughter echoes. Everything that is obscene or pornographic the *favelado* learns quickly.

There are some shacks where prostitutes play their love scenes right in front of the children.

The rich neighbors in the brick houses say we are protected by the politicians. They're wrong. The politicians only show up here in the Garbage Dump at election time. This year we had a visit from a candidate for deputy, Dr. Paulo de Campos Moura, who gave us beans and some wonderful blankets. He came at an opportune moment, before it got cold.

What I want to clear up about the people who live in the favela is the following: the only ones who really survive here are the *nordestinos*.[13] They work and don't squander. They buy a house or go back up north.

Here in the favela there are those who build shacks to live

---

[13] *Nordestinos*: forced by land-parching droughts and almost no industry, the poor of the north swarm into cities like São Paulo and Rio looking for work. Needing a place to live, they choose the favelas and end up worse off than they were before.

in and those who build them to rent. And the rents are from 500 to 700 cruzeiros. Those who make shacks to sell spend 4,000 cruzeiros and sell them for 11,000. Who made a lot of shacks to sell was Tiburcio.

May 29 It finally stopped raining. The clouds glided toward the horizon. Only the cold attacked us. Many people in the favela don't have warm clothing. When one has shoes he won't have a coat. I choke up watching the children walk in the mud. It seems that some new people have arrived in the favela. They are ragged with undernourished faces. They improvised a shack. It hurts me to see so much pain, reserved for the working class. I stared at my new companion in misfortune. She looked at the favela with its mud and sickly children. It was the saddest look I'd ever seen. Perhaps she has no more illusions. She had given her life over to misery.

There will be those who reading what I write will say—this is untrue. But misery is real.

What I revolt against is the greed of men who squeeze other men as if they were squeezing oranges.

May 30 I changed Vera's clothes and we went out. Then I thought: I wonder if God is going to have pity on me? I wonder if I will get any money today? I wonder if God knows the favelas exist and that the *favelados* are hungry?

José Carlos came home with a bag of crackers he found in the garbage. When I saw him eating things out of the trash I thought: and if it's been poisoned? Children can't stand hunger. The crackers were delicious. I ate them thinking of that proverb: He who enters the dance must dance. And as I also was hungry, I ate.

More new people arrived in the favela. They are shabby and walk bent over with their eyes on the ground as if doing penance for their misfortune of living in an ugly place. A place where you can't plant one flower to breathe its perfume. To listen to the buzz of the bees or watch a hummingbird caressing the flower with his fragile beak. The only perfume that comes from the favela is from rotting mud, excrement, and whisky.

Today nobody is going to sleep because the *favelados* who don't work have started to dance. Cans, frying pans, pots —everything serves to accompany the off-key singing of these night bums.

May 31 Saturday—a day that always drives me crazy because I have to arrange for something to eat for both Satur-

day and Sunday. I made breakfast using the bread that I got
yesterday. I put beans on the fire. When I was washing the
beans I thought: today I feel like Society—I'm going to cook
beans! It seemed like a dream.

I got some bananas and manioc roots at a shop on
Guaporé Street. When I was returning to the favela a lady
at 728 Avenue Cruzeiro do Sul asked me to throw a dead dog
into the Tieté and she would give me five cruzeiros. I left
Vera with her and went. The dog was inside a bag. The
woman stood watching my *"Paulistana"* steps. That means
walking fast. When I returned she gave me six cruzeiros.
When I received the money I thought: now I've got enough
to buy some soap.

I arrived in the favela: I don't think I can say I arrived in
my house. A house is a house. A shack is a shack. The shack,
as much interior as exterior, was dirty. That mess disgusts me.
I stared at the yard. The rotting garbage was stinking. Only
on Sundays do I have time to clean.

I had bought an egg and 15 cruzeiros of pork at Senhor
Eduardo. I fried the egg to see if it would stop my nausea.
It did. I felt weak. The doctor told me to eat olive oil but
I can't afford it. I made dinner. Rice, beans, pepper, a sau-
sage, and fried mandioca. When Vera saw so many things
she said: today is a Negro's holiday!

I asked a woman that I saw for the first time:

"Are you living here?"

"I am, but pretend I'm not, because I can't stand this
place. This is a place for pigs. But if they put pigs in here
they would complain and go on strike. I always heard people
talk of the favela but I never dreamed it would be a place as
loathsome as this. Only God has pity on us."

June 1 The beginning of the month. The year is slipping
away. A person sees his friends die and others born. It's
3:30 in the morning. I can't sleep. That Victor showed up, the
ugliest man in the favela. A representative for the bogey-
man. He's so ugly, yet he's got two women. When he came
to live in the favela he started showing off, saying:

"I was vaccinated with the blood of *Lampeão!*" [14]

The first of January 1958 he told me he was going to
bust my head. But I taught him that A was A and B was B.

[14] Lampeão: a bandit leader who terrorized the northeast of
Brazil, robbing, raping, and murdering wantonly until tracked
down and beheaded by state militia.

He is like iron and I'm like steel. I don't have any physical force but my words hurt more than a sword. And the wounds don't heal. He stopped bothering me because I called the Radio Patrol on him, and he spent four hours locked up. When he got out he walked around saying he was going to kill me. Then Adalberto told him:

"Talking like that is the worst thing you could do. Because if you don't kill her, she is going to kill you."

I have an ability that I'm not going to talk about here, because it has to defend me. Who lives in the favela must try and isolate themselves—live alone. Victor is playing the radio. I thought: today is Sunday and we can sleep until 8. But here there is no consideration.

I haven't said anything about my dear mother. She was very good. She wanted me to study to be a teacher. It was the uncertainties of life that made it impossible for her to realize her dream. But she formed my character, taught me to like the humble and the weak. That's why I have pity on the *favelados.* I know very well that there are contemptible people here, persons with perverted souls. Last night Amelia and her companion fought. She told him that he was with her only for the money she gave him. You only had to listen to Amelia's voice to know she enjoyed the argument. She had many children. Gave them all away. She has two boys at home that she doesn't want. She neglects children and collects men.

A man enters by the door. A child is the root of the heart.

It's 4 o'clock—I've just made lunch. Today there was lunch. We had rice, beans, cabbage, and sausage. When I cook four dishes I think that I'm really someone. When I see my children eating rice and beans, food that is not in reach of the *favelado,* I smile stupidly. As if I was watching a dazzling display. I washed the clothes and the shack. Now I'm going to read and write. I watched the young boys playing ball. They run around the field showing off their energy. I think: if they could drink fresh milk and eat meat . . .

June 2 It dawned cold. I lit a fire and sent João to buy bread and coffee. Chico at the market cut off a piece of the bread.

I cursed Chico for being common and a dog, and I wanted to be a thunderbolt to shatter him into a thousand pieces. The bread didn't go around and the boys didn't take any lunch to school.

In the morning I'm always nervous. I'm afraid of not getting money to buy food to eat. But today is Monday and there is a lot of paper in the streets. Senhor Manuel showed up saying he wanted to marry me. But I don't want to, because I'm in my maturity. And later a man isn't going to like a woman who can't stop reading and gets out of bed to write and sleeps with paper and pencil under her pillow. That's why I prefer to live alone, for my ideals. He gave me 50 cruzeiros and I paid the seamstress for a dress that she made for Vera. Dona Alice came by complaining that Senhor Alexandre was insulting her because of 65 cruzeiros. I thought: ah money! It kills and it makes hate take root.

June 3   When I was at the streetcar stop Vera started to cry. She wanted a cookie. I only had ten cruzeiros, two for the streetcar and eight to buy hamburger. Dona Geralda gave me four cruzeiros for me to buy the cookies. She ate and sang. I thought: my problem is always food! I took the streetcar and Vera started to cry because she didn't want to stand up, and there wasn't any place to sit down.

When I have little money I try not to think of children who are going to ask for bread. Bread and coffee. I sent my thoughts toward the sky. I thought: can it be that people live up there? Are they better than us? Can it be that they have an advantage over us? Can it be that nations up there are as different as nations on earth? Or is there just one nation? I wonder if the favela exists there? And if up there a favela does exist, can it be that when I die I'm going to live in a favela?

When I started to write I heard angry voices. It's been a long time since there has been a fight in the favela. It was Odete and her husband Alcino, who is separated. They fought because he brought another woman in the car he is working on. They were in the house of Francisco, Alcino's brother. They went into the street and I went to see the fight. They attacked the woman that was with Alcino. Four women and a boy pushed the woman with such a violence that she fell to the ground. Marli left, saying she was going to find a rock to throw at that woman's head. I put the woman in the car and told Alcino to take her away. I thought of going to call the police. But before the police would come they would have killed the woman. Alcino gave a few slaps to his mother-in-law, who was the worst of the troublemakers. If I hadn't come to the aid of Alcino he would have been outnumbered. The women of a favela are horrible in a fight. Things that could be solved with words they transform into fists. They act like buzzards in a fight.

Odete was furious with me for having defended Alcino. I said:

"You have four children to take care of."

"I don't care. I wanted to kill her."

When I shoved the woman into the car, she said to me: "You are the only kind one here."

I had the impression I was taking away a bone from the mouths of dogs. And when Odete saw her husband leaving with the other woman in the car she was furious. She turned on me and criticized me for being a meddler. I don't think that violence ever resolves anything. A Congress of *favelados* is with clubs, knives, stones, and violence.

A favela is a room of surprises. This is the fifth woman that Alcino has brought here, and when his wife sees them there is always a fight. Today the favela is hot. During the day Leila and her companion Arnaldo fought. Arnaldo is black. When he came to the favela he was a boy. But what a boy. He was kind, educated, gentle, and obedient. He was the pride of his father and all those who knew him.

"This is going to be a Negro, yes sir!"

In Africa the Negroes are classified like this:

Negro tu.

Negro turututu.

And Negro, yes sir!

Negro tu is a regular Negro. Negro turututu is one who's not worth anything. But a Negro, yes sir! is high society. But Arnaldo turned into a Negro turututu after he grew up. He became stupid, pornographic, obscene, and alcoholic. I don't know how anybody could destroy himself like that. He is Godfather for Dona Domingas.

But what a Godfather!

Dona Domingas is a black as good as bread. Calm and helpful. When Leila didn't have a house she went to live with Dona Domingas.

Dona Domingas washed all the clothes and Leila forced her to give up her bed and sleep on the floor. Leila became boss in the house. I said:

"Rebel, Domingas!"

"She's a witch. She could put a curse on me."

"But there's no such thing as a witch."

"Yes there is and she is one. I've seen her do it."

That's why Leila was going around saying she mended lives. And I saw many rich women show up here. There was that Dona Guiomar or Edviges Gonçalves, a woman who has many names and many addresses because she buys on credit and never pays and changes her name every time she buys. When she walks down the street she thinks she's Marie Antoinette. Dona Guiomar agreed to the enslaving of Dona Domingas. Dona Domingas receives a pension from her dead husband. She was forced to give money to Leila, Arnaldo's companion. He being Domingas' Godfather was supposed to take care of his godchild. But he exploited her. He divided her money between them. They even practiced their love scenes in front of her son.

Dona Domingas left the house. She went to the town of Carapicuiba to live with Dona Iracema. Her son Nilton stayed. I did everything I could to take the boy away, but Leila had told him:

"I'm a witch and if you go away, I'll turn you into an elephant."

I met Nilton:

"Hello, Nilton, don't you want to go to your mother?"

"I can't go because Leila told me she's a witch and if I go away she will turn me into an elephant, and an elephant is a very ugly animal. Do you know, Dona Carolina, if she can turn me into a pig? I'd have to eat garbage and someone would put me into a pigsty so I would get fat. They'd cut my balls off. And if she makes me turn into a horse someone would take me and make me pull a cart and they'd beat me with a whip."

When Nilton started to go hungry he went to his mother. I thought: hunger acts as a judge.

One day I argued with Leila. She and Arnaldo set fire to my shack. The neighbors put it out.

June 5 I have now observed our politicians. To watch them I went to Congress. A branch of Purgatory, for it's the head office of the Social Service, in the Governor's Palace. What I saw there made me gnash my teeth. I saw the poor go out crying. The tears of the poor stir the poets. They don't move the poets of the living room, but they do move the poet of the garbage dump, this idealist of the favela, a spectator who sees and notes the tragedies that the politicians inflict on the people.

June 6 For days José Carlos hasn't stayed home. When he comes in to sleep, it's 10:30 at night. This morning he got it. I told him that if he returned after 10:00 I wasn't going to open the door. I bought bread at 2 p.m. At 5 p.m. a piece was already hard. Bread is just like the heart of a politician. Hard in the face of human need.

Today there was a fight here in the favela. They fought over a dog. The fight was among some *Baianos*,[15] who only speak in knives.

June 7 The boys drank some coffee and went to school. They are happy because today there is coffee. Only those who have gone hungry know the value of food.

Vera and I went to look for paper. We passed the slaughterhouse to beg for some sausage. I counted nine women in line. I have a mania to observe everything, tell everything, and note down the facts.

I found a lot of paper in the streets and got 20 cruzeiros. I went to a bar and had coffee and milk. One for me and another for Vera. I spent 11 cruzeiros. I kept on looking for paper until 11:30 at night, and earned another 50 cruzeiros.

When I was a girl my dream was to be a man to defend Brazil, because I read the history of Brazil and became aware that war existed. I read the masculine names of the defenders of the country, then I said to my mother:

"Why don't you make me become a man?"

She replied:

"If you walk under a rainbow, you'll become a man."

When a rainbow appeared I went running in its direction. But the rainbow was always a long way off. Just as the politicians are a long way off from the people. I got tired and sat down. Afterward I started to cry. But the people must not get tired. They must not cry. They must fight to improve Brazil so that our children don't suffer as we are suffering. I returned and told my mother:

"The rainbow ran away from me."

We are poor, and we live on the banks of the river. The river banks are places for garbage and the marginal people. People of the favelas are considered marginals. No more do you see buzzards flying the river banks near the trash. The unemployed have taken the buzzards' place.

When I went out to look for paper I met a black. He was

---

[15] *Baianos:* people from the state of Bahia.

ragged and dirty and I felt sorry for him. In his tattered clothes he could pass for the president of the Unfortunates' Union. In his eyes there was an anguished look as if he had seen all the misery of the world. He was unworthy of being human. He was eating some candy that a factory had thrown into the dirt. He wiped off the mud and ate the candy. He wasn't drunk but staggered when he walked. He was dizzy from hunger.

I met him another time, near the place where I take the paper, and I told him:

"You wait here. I'm going to sell this paper and will give you five cruzeiros so you can have some coffee. It's good to drink a little coffee in the morning."

"I don't want it. You haul those papers around with great difficulty so you can support your children. You only get a crumb, yet you want to share it with me. This work that you do is work for a horse. I know what I'm going to do with my life. In a few more days I'm not going to need anything more in this world. I can't live on a farm. The farmers exploit me too much. I can't live in the city because everything here is money and I can't find a job because I'm old. I know I'm going to die of hunger, the worst of the illnesses."

The man stopped talking, suddenly. I went on with the sack of paper on my back.

There are people who go to a dance every Saturday. I don't dance. I think it's ridiculous to keep turning this way, then that. I have to twist and turn too much just to get money to eat.

I looked for Vera and didn't find her. I shouted, she didn't appear. I went to the Portuguese Sport Club, they are starting their June festival. She wasn't there. I went to the streetcar stop three times. I was even thinking of going to juvenile court, spending all the money I had saved for bread. When I returned to the favela for my documents, so I could go to the city, Vera was looking for me. She told me she had gone hunting for balloons. I was exhausted from running.

June 8 Today I fixed lunch. When there is meat, I'm alive. But when there is just cornmeal, I know I'm going to have trouble with the children. Beans, rice, and pastry. For a long time the boys have been asking for pastry. João is smiling foolishly. Pastry is an event in this house.

When I say house I feel that I'm offending the brick homes. Today the *favelados* are enjoying the troublemakers. They are two brothers, Vicente and João Coque. There, in front of the market the two *Baianos* . . . two brothers . . . are fighting. You'd never know they were from the same womb.

The neighbors in the brick houses look at the *favelados* with disgust. I see their looks of hate because they don't want the favela here. They say the favela debases the neighborhood and that they despise poverty. They forget that in death everyone is poor.

All I know is, whatever is cursed, the *favelado* gets. When we moved into the favela we went to ask for water from the brick houses. Dona Ida Cardoso gave us water. Thirteen times she gave us water. She told us she'd only give us water on weekdays; on Sunday she wanted to sleep late. The *favelado* is not a donkey but he was vaccinated with donkey's blood. One day they went to get water and didn't find the public spigot turned on. So they formed a line at the door of Dona Ida and everybody shouted:

"I want water for the baby's bottle. My God, what are we going to do without water?"

They went to other houses, beating on the doors. Nobody answered. Nobody showed up to wait on them, so not to listen to:

"Could you give us a little water?"

I carried water from Guaporé Street from the place where I sell paper. Others carried water from the Social Service in bottles.

One Tuesday afternoon Dona Ida's mother-in-law was sitting resting and she said:

"Somebody should send a flood to wipe away the favela and kill those nuisances. There are times when I'm furious with God for putting poor people on earth. All they do is annoy others."

Tina, Dona Mulata's daughter, when she knew that Dona Ida's mother-in-law had asked God to send a flood to kill the poor *favelados,* said:

"If anyone should die drowning, it should be her!"

In the flood of '49, Pedro Cardoso died. He was Dona Ida's son. When I heard that little Pedro had died by drowning I thought of the disappointment his grandmother must have had asking for water, water, enough water to kill the *favelados* and then seeing water kill her grandson. It was for her to understand that God is temperate. He is the lawyer of the humble. The poor are creatures of God. And money is a metal created and valued by man. If God had warned Dona Ida that if she didn't give us water, she would lose her child forever, I believe she would be giving us water until today. Pedro was a self-sacrifice to the pride of his grandmother, and the evil of his mother. That is how God punishes.

June 9 I went out. When I was looking for paper in front of Bela Vista I had the feeling that I was going to have trouble. When I was passing Pedro Vicente Street a man gave a rubber ball to Vera. She was happy and told the man that he could go to Heaven.

When Vera was born I was alone in the favela. No woman showed up to wash my clothes or look after my children. My boys slept filthy. I stayed in bed thinking of my boys, afraid for them playing on the river bank. After a birth a woman doesn't have strength to lift an arm. After the birth I stayed in an uncomfortable position until God gave me the strength to arrange myself.

I was lying down when I heard children's voices shouting they were showing a free movie in the street. I didn't believe what I heard and decided to go and see. It was the health department. They came to show a film to the *favelados* on how snails transmit anemic disease. They told us not to use the river water. That young snails grow up in that water. Even the water . . . instead of helping us, it contaminates us. Not even the air we breathe is pure, because they throw garbage here in the favela.

They asked the *favelados* to build bathrooms!

June 11 It's now six months that I haven't paid for water at 25 cruzeiros a month. Speaking of water, I don't like, and have a fear of, going for water. When the women conglomerate at the spigot, when they're waiting their turn to fill their cans, they talk of everybody and everything. If a woman is getting fat they say she's pregnant. If she's losing weight they say she has tuberculosis. We have a Dona Binidita here, who is 82 years old. She started to put on weight.

"Dona Binidita is pregnant!"

"You don't say! At that age?"

"That is too much!"

"How many months?"

Six, seven, the date changes with the lie. And when someone took some baby clothes to Dona Binidita she shouted and cursed:

"I am one mother who has long been out of circulation. How I can have a baby? I've retired!"

When I heard the rumors I thought: the only woman who could have children at this age was Saint Isabel, the mother of John the Baptist.

Every day there is something new here in the favela. When the Portuguese Sport Club was opened, the Portuguese who live near here went. Dona Isaltina left some clothes in her yard. The next day she didn't find them. Dona Sebastiana called the Radio Patrol. They questioned Leila with such force that they ended up finding the clothes at the bottom of a cesspool. They took a stick and fished out the clothes. And the police forced Leila to wash them. A truck from the mayor's office came with water, and threw water while Lelia washed. She said:

"It wasn't me who took these clothes. I'm a whore, but I'm not a thief!"

The people of the favela always find time to be present at these shows. A judge picked up a young mental case. They said she had run off with a Japanese. Today she came back and said it was a lie.

I went to Dona Julita's. She gave me coffee, soup, and bread. At 1140 State Street I got a lot of paper. I received 98 cruzeiros. It was enough to buy oil, meat, and sugar. I found some bananas and made dessert. José Carlos was much calmer after I squeezed out his worms. Twenty-one worms. *June 12* I left the bed at 3 a.m. because when one is not sleepy he starts to think of the misery around him. I got out of bed to write. When I write I think I live in a golden castle that shines in the sunlight. The windows are silver and the panes are diamonds. My view is overlooking a garden and I gaze on flowers of all kinds. I must create this atmosphere of fantasy to forget that I am in a favela.

I made coffee and went for water. The stars were in the heavens. How disgusting it is to step in mud.

My happy hours are when I am living in my imaginary castles.

That Valdemar today attacked Senhor Alexandre with a hoe. Some women intervened. I admired Alexandre's courage in facing Valdemar. The braver women of the favela slapped Valdemar with their brooms and sandals. But when someone is afraid of him, he wins.

June 13 I dressed the boys and they went to school. I went to look for paper. At the slaughterhouse I saw a young girl eating sausages from the garbage.

"You should get yourself a job and you'd have a better life."

She asked me if looking for paper earned money. I told her it did. She said she wanted to work so she could walk around looking pretty. She was 15 years old, the age when we think the world is wonderful. The age when the rose unfolds. Later it falls petal by petal and leaves just the thorns. For those who tire of life . . . there is suicide. Others steal. I looked at the face of the girl. She had blisters all over her mouth.

The prices mount up like waves of the sea. Each one is stronger. Who fights with waves? Only the sharks. But the strongest shark is the thinking one. He walks on earth. He is the merchant.[16]

Lentils are 100 cruzeiros a kilo, a fact that pleases me immensely. I danced, sang and jumped and thanked God, the judge of kings! Where am I to get 100 cruzeiros? It was in January when the waters flooded the warehouses and ruined the food. Well done. Rather than sell the things cheaply, they kept them waiting for higher prices. I saw men throw sacks of rice into the river. They threw dried codfish, cheese, and sweets. How I envied the fish who didn't work but lived better than I.

Today I am reading. I read about the crime of Nei Maranhão, a deputy in Recife. I read aloud so the favela women could hear. They became furious and started to rail against the murderer. They prayed for a curse on him. I have seen what curses the *favelados* pray for.

The good I praise, the evil I criticize. I must reserve my soft words for the workers, for the beggars, who are the slaves of misery.

June 14 It's raining and I can't go out looking for paper. On a rainy day I'm a beggar. I walk around ragged and dirty. I wear the uniform of the unfortunate. And today is Saturday. The *favelados* are considered beggars and I'm going to take advantage of it. Vera can't go with me because of the rain. I dug out an old umbrella that I found in the garbage and went out. At the slaughterhouse I got some bones. They'll

---

[16] In Portuguese slang, shark is the name given to anyone who tries to make high or illicit profits from others.

do to make soup. At least the stomach won't remain empty. I've tried to live on air and almost fainted. I resolved then and there to work because I don't want to give up this life.

I'd like to see how I'm going to die. Nobody should feed the idea of suicide. But today he who lives till the hour of his death is a hero. Because he who is not strong gives in.

I heard a woman complaining that the bones she got at the slaughterhouse were clean.

"And I like meat so much!"

I got nervous listening to the woman complaining because it's hard enough for people just to live on this earth, not having sufficient food to eat. For as I've noted, God is the king of the wise men. He put men and animals on the earth. But what the animals eat, nature supplies. If animals had to eat like men, they would suffer greatly. I think of this because when I have nothing to eat I envy the animals.

When I was waiting in line to get some crackers, I listened to the women complaining. One told of stopping at a house and asking for a handout. The lady of the house told her to wait. The woman said that the housewife came back with a package and gave it to her. She didn't want to open the package near her friends, because they would ask for some of it. She started to think. Is it a piece of cheese? Can it be meat? When she got back to her shack, the first thing she did was tear open the package. When she unwrapped it, out fell two dead rats.

There are people who make fun of those who beg. The man said he wouldn't give out any more crackers, but the women remained calm. And the line grew. When a customer arrived to buy, he explained:

"Excuse the ugliness of these people waiting at the factory door. It's my bad luck that every Saturday they put me through this hell."

I waited impatiently to hear what else the factory owner would say. I wanted to hear what the women said. What a sad sight for those who were present. The poor wanting something. The rich not wanting to give. He handed out only pieces of crackers. And they were as happy as Queen Elizabeth of England when she received the 13 millions in jewels that President Kubitschek sent her as a birthday present.

The factory owner, seeing that they didn't go away, ordered them given whole crackers. An employee gave them to us and said:

"Everyone who gets his crackers must get away from here."

They claim that they're not able to give alms because the price of the wheat flour had gone up a great deal. But the beggars are now in the habit of getting their crackers every Saturday.

I didn't get any crackers so I went to the street market to pick up vegetables. I met Dona Maria do José Bento and we started to talk about the cost of living.

June 15 I bought meat, bread, and soap. I stopped at a news-stand. I read that a woman with three children had committed suicide because she found it too difficult to live. The woman who killed herself didn't have the soul of a *favelado*, who when in hunger goes through garbage, picks up vegetables from the street fair, begs and keeps on living. The poor woman! Who knows how long she had been thinking of killing herself, because mothers worry a good deal for their children. But what a shame against a nation. A person who kills herself because of hunger. The worst thing that a mother can hear is the symphony:

"Mama, I want some bread! Mama, I'm hungry!"

I thought: did she go to the Social Service? She should have gone inside the palaces to talk to the men who pull the strings.

The item in the newspaper left me nervous. I spent the whole day cursing the politicians because I as well, when I don't have anything to give to my children, almost go crazy.

Here in the favela there is a soccer team—The Blacks and Reds. Their shirts are black and red. The organizer is Almiro Castilho. The team is not known to the public. Two years ago, the team went to play in Penha. And argued with their op-posing team and the argument turned into a battle. Only with the intervention of the police did the argument stop. There was one dead and various wounded. Nobody went to prison but investigations were started. Everyone of them had to pay 2,000 cruzeiros to a lawyer.

Today there was a fight. On "A" Street live ten Bahians in one shack eight by ten feet. Five are brothers. And the other five are sisters. They are strong and evil-looking. Men who would have been of value for Lampeão. There are another ten who are *Pernambucanos*. And those ten fought with one *Paraibano*.[17] When the *Pernambucanos* went for the *Parai-*

---

[17] *Paraibanos:* people from the northern State of Paraíba.

bano, the women grabbed him, carried him inside the shack, and locked the door. The *Pernambucanos* kept saying they would kill and carve up the *Paraibano*. They wanted to invade the shack. They were as furious as a pack of dogs when you take away their bitch.

She had six children: three by Maról̇o and three by others. She had a boy that might have been four years old. But one day they all got drunk, and argued and fought inside the house. The battle was terrific. The shack began to tremble. And the pots fell noisily. In the confusion the boy fell on the floor and was stepped on. Everybody thought the boy was completely broken. Finally they took him to the clinic. They put him into a plaster cast. But the bones did not set. The boy died.

Now she is with two girls. One of two years and the other just born. Her present companion drinks and fights. And at times they roll on the floor. When I see these things I keep thinking of the boy who died.

There was a soldier who showed up here. He tried to make me. And I ran away from him. I fell for his foolishness and told Leila that I thought the soldier was very handsome, but I didn't want anything to do with him because he drank *pinga*. One day he came around to talk to me, stinking of *pinga*. Then one night he appeared and said to me:

"Hey, Dona Carolina, why are you going around saying that I drink *pinga*?"

I thought immediately of Leila, because I had said that only to her. I answered:

"I think you are handsome, but I'm afraid of men who drink *pinga*."

I could see that he didn't appreciate my remark.

"Don't you know that a German soldier isn't allowed to drink?" I told him.

He looked at me and said:

"Then thank God I'm a Brazilian!"

June 16 José Carlos is feeling better. I gave him a garlic enema and some hortelã tea. I scoff at women's medicine but I had to give it to him because actually you've got to arrange things the best you can. Due to the cost of living we have to return to the primitive, wash in tubs, cook with wood.

I wrote plays and showed them to directors of circuses. They told me:

"It's a shame you're black."

They were forgetting that I adore my black skin and my kinky hair. The Negro hair is more educated than the white man's hair. Because with Negro hair, where you put it, it stays. It's obedient. The hair of the white, just give one quick movement, and it's out of place. It won't obey. If reincarnation exists I want to come back black.

One day a white told me:

"If the blacks had arrived on earth after the whites, then the whites would have complained and rightly so. But neither the white nor the black knows its origin."

The white man says he is superior. But what superiority does he show? If the Negro drinks *pinga,* the white drinks. The sickness that hits the black hits the white. If the white feels hunger, so does the Negro. Nature hasn't picked any favorites.

June 17 I spent the night like this: I woke up and wrote. Afterward I went back to sleep. At 5 a.m. Vera started to vomit. I gave her some medicine, she slept. When the rain stopped I took advantage of it and went out. I filled one sack with paper. I only received 12 cruzeiros. I found some tomatoes and a little garlic and ran home because Vera is sick. When I arrived she was sleeping. But with the noise I made she woke up. She said she was hungry. I bought some milk and made oatmeal for her. She ate, then vomited up a worm. Afterward she got up, walked a bit, then laid down again.

I went to Senhor Manuel to sell some iron and get money. I am nervous with fear Vera will get worse, because the money I have will not be enough to pay a doctor. Today I am praying and begging God that Vera gets better.

June 18 Today it dawned raining. Yesterday Vera spit two worms out of her mouth. She has a fever. There is no school today in honor of the Prince of Japan.

June 19 Vera is still sick. She told me it was the garlic enema I gave her that made her ill. But here in the favela various children are attacked by worms.

José Carlos doesn't want to go to school because it is getting cold and he doesn't have shoes. But today is exam day and he went. I am worried because the cold is freezing. But what can I do?

I left and went to hunt paper. I passed by Dona Julita's but she was at the market. I went by the shoe store to collect their paper. The sack was heavy. I should have carried the paper in two trips. But I carried it in one because I wanted to get home sooner because Vera was sick and alone.

June 20 I gave Vera some milk. All I know is that milk is an extra expense and is ruining my unhappy pocketbook. I put Vera to bed and went out. I was so nervous! I felt I was as a battlefield where no one was going to get out alive. I thought of the clothes I had to wash and of Vera. If she gets worse? I can't possibly count on her father. He doesn't know Vera, nor has Vera ever seen him.

Everything in my life is fantastic. Father doesn't know his child, the child doesn't know his father.

There was no paper in the streets. And I wanted to buy a pair of shoes for Vera. I went on looking for paper. I earned 41 cruzeiros. I kept thinking of Vera, who would complain and cry because when she doesn't have anything to wear, she sobs that she doesn't like to be poor. I thought: if misery even revolts children . . .

June 21 I dressed José Carlos to send him to school. When I was in the street I got nervous. Every day it's the same fight. I walk like an aimless Jew after money, and the money that I get doesn't buy anything. I went by the slaughterhouse and got some bones. When I left this morning Vera asked me to bring her some shoes. I left João playing with her because today there is no school for the second grade. I went up many streets and there wasn't any paper. When I got 30 cruzeiros I thought: this will just pay for Vera's shoes. But it was Saturday and I needed money for Sunday and Vera had already started dreaming up a Sunday menu. On Tiradentes Avenue I got some roofing tiles and sold them at the yard of Senhor Salvador Zanutti on Voluntarios da Patria Street. I am angry with him even though he never did anything to me. He even lent me money once when I was sick. When I am sick I walk around wanting to kill myself for lack of money.

Senhor Salvador asked me why I had disappeared. I was ashamed with his friendly greeting. He gave me 31 cruzeiros. Oh, I was happy! I ran to buy shoes for Vera. Then I remembered that I had left my bag at the yard. Traffic was thick. I managed to cross and get the sack. He said to me:

"You ran away and forgot your sack."

I picked up a little more paper and got ten cruzeiros. Thus I had 71 cruzeiros. I gave 30 cruzeiros for the shoes and kept 41. It wasn't going to be enough to buy coffee, bread, sugar, rice, and lard. I thought of the bones. I would make soup. I

have a little rice and a little macaroni and I mixed everything and made soup. If Vera wants to eat, then let her eat;
if she doesn't want to, then it's nobody's fault but her own.
Nowadays nobody can afford to have preferences or be
squeamish. I hurried home to see how she was. She was
playing. I thought: now she's getting better.

She was scratching herself and her skin was irritated. I
think it was the garlic enema I gave her. I swear never again
to give medicine recommended by scrubwomen in hospitals.
I showed her the shoes and she became happy. She smiled
and said to me: that she was happy with me and wasn't going
to buy a white mother. That I didn't lie. That I said I would
buy shoes and I bought them. That I kept my word.

I was so tired. I wanted to go and try to get more
money. But exhaustion dominated me. I heard the children
shouting that they were giving out cards. I sped like an
arrow, the tiredness gone. I met João who was waving a
card in his hand. All of them were smiling as if they had
won a prize. I read the card. It was to go and get "a prize and
a surprise for your child at Javais Street No. 771."

June 22 I got out of bed at 5 o'clock, preparing the children
for the party at Javais Street. I gave food to Vera. João
didn't want my food. He said:

"I'm going to eat at the party. The food there must be
better than yours."

He doesn't like parties. But if he knows there is going to
be food then he's the first to insist we take an empty bag. I
passed by Dona Julita's to tell her we were going to the
party. I thought: it must be a banquet because St. Louis
King of France, when he invited the public to eat, prepared
a banquet. I took the streetcar. I didn't have enough money. I
arrived at 2 o'clock. The line was enormous. There must have
been 3,000 people. When they came with the invitations the
favelados were delighted. Those who didn't get a card cried
and said they were unlucky. The people of the favela like
handouts. They put some boards on the sidewalk, covered
them with newspapers, then put bread on top. I heard a
woman say:

"It's not so bad to be poor."

They were all shabbily dressed. Some wore shoes, others
barefoot. Then a black man appeared, tall and fat, as if he
was descended from the elephants. He spoke so all could
hear.

"I am not a deputy. I am simply a friend of the poor."

I started to write down what I was seeing in that conglomeration. Because I am tall and was dressed all in red, Senhor Zuza saw me writing. I went to talk to him. I asked:

"Who are you?"

"Man! I am Zuza! The senhora never heard people speak of Zuza? But Zuza is me!"

"Why are you giving this party?"

"I am giving this party for the people."

"I'm going to put you in my book."

"You can put me wherever you want!"

I didn't like that Zuza. There is something lacking there that keeps him from being a complete man. He, noting the impatience of the people, said:

"Wait! Are you all dying of hunger?"

I saw a pregnant woman faint. Zuza gave some bread to the woman, then ordered them to wave the bread in the air, for the photographer. The cars and buses had trouble trying to go down a street that had children running from one side to the other. I expected one of them to get hit any minute. Some were complaining:

"If I had known it was only going to be bread, I wouldn't have come."

Senhor Zuza had two guitarists play and a clown showed up. What a disgusting party.

It was Sunday and people were shocked to see beggars crowding on the Bom Retiro bus. Coming over we were lucky. We found a conductor who accepted whatever we gave him. Some gave one cruzeiro, others he just let pass. There was a woman with children who had come from Santos (50 miles away) and got only one bread, a little bag of candy, and a school ruler that had written on it "Remembrance of Deputy Paulo Teixeira de Camargo."

There was a woman who had spent 20 cruzeiros on transportation. And she didn't get anything. The line was in the shade and it was cold. I got out of line and went to the other side. I must have scared Senhor Zuza for he gave me many bread rolls. I counted six. Then I stopped him and asked God not to let him give me any more. I heard many women cursing him. We were lucky on the return trip too. It was the same conductor. I had five children and, counting myself, six. That's why I had to beg the conductor to let us ride for three cruzeiros. It was all the money I had. And Vera's feet had swelled from so much walking. When I got back to the favela I heard women praying curses on Zuza. Most women with children didn't get any bread because they didn't get into the middle of the mob that was saying:

"Let's get some of that bread so the trip isn't completely wasted."

I found Senhor Alexandre fighting with Vicente over a ruler he loaned him.

It was 6 o'clock when a car appeared. There was a man who had gotten married and his friends came to give us the left-over sandwiches. I got some. Then the *favelados* invaded the car. The boys drove off saying they were going to throw the sandwiches in the garbage because the people of the favela were stupid four-legged beasts that needed harnesses not sandwiches.

June 23 I stopped at the butcher to buy a half kilo of beef. The prices were 24 and 28. I was confused about the differences in prices. The butcher explained to me that filet was more expensive. I thought of the bad luck of the cow, the slave of man. Those that live in the woods eat vegetation, they like salt, but man doesn't give it because it's too expensive. After death they are divided, weighed, and selected. And they die when man wants them to. In life they give money to man. Their death enriches the man. Actually, the world is the way the whites want it. I'm not white, so I don't have anything to do with this disorganized world.

When I got back to the favela the children were playing. I asked if anyone had fought with them. They said only the *Baiana,* a neighbor that has three children. And that Leila fought with Arnaldo and wanted to throw their newborn daughter into the Tieté River. They fought all the way to Port Street. And Leila threw the child on the ground. The little girl is only two months old. The women wanted to call the police and take the baby to the police orphanage. I was tired and laid down. I didn't even have the strength to take off my clothes.

June 24 When I returned to the favela I found Vera in the street. She tells me everything that goes on. She said the police had come to tell Paredão that his mother was dead.

She was a very good woman. Only she drank too much.

I was giving lunch when Vera came to tell me there was a fight in the favela. I went to see. It was Maria Mathias who was giving one of her hysterical spectaculars. A spectacular at the critical age. Only women and doctors will understand what I mean.

Every year the *favelados* make bonfires. To honor St. Anthony, St. John, and St. Peter on their special days. But instead of finding their own kindling they rob from others. They enter yards and carry off wood belonging to others. I had a ceiling beam. They took it to burn. I don't know why it is that the *favelados* are so destructive. It's not enough that they don't have any good qualities, but bad characters show up around here to make things worse. The principal troublemakers here are Chico, Bom Bril, and Valdemar. Valdemar gets up in the morning and comes to the favela.

Why doesn't this man go to work? He hates me. I like his mother very much. But Dona Aparecida told me it was the *favelados* who corrupted her son. Few of the favela men go to work. The others that don't work loaf around all day. Nobody asks Valdemar to come here. He was just born with a low character. Ah, if one could write only praise! If I write that Valdemar is a good guy and someone who knows him reads it, they'll not believe anything I'd ever write again.

I sat down near the bonfire. Joaquim and his wife Pitita were fighting. Poor Joaquim. He shows the greatest of patience in not leaving home.

June 25 I made coffee and dressed the children for school. I put beans on to cook. I dressed Vera and we went out. João was playing. When he saw me, he ran. And José Carlos gets frightened when he hears my voice. I saw a government station wagon. The São Paulo Health Department had come to pick up the excrement. The papers say there are 160 positive worm cases here in the favela. Is it possible they're going to give away medicine? The majority of the *favelados* don't have any way to buy it. I didn't take the examination. I went to look for paper. I only got 25 cruzeiros. And now there is a man who looks for paper in my zone. But I didn't fight with him over it. Because in a few days he'll give up. He is already complaining that what he gets doesn't even go to buy *pinga*. That it's better to beg.

I went past the canning factory and found a few tomatoes. The manager when he saw me began to swear at me. But the poor must pretend that they can't hear. When I got home I made a salad for the children.

I heard some kids saying there was a fight. I went to see. It was Nair and Meiry. Nair is white. Meiry is black. For quite

a while now Meiry has been going around saying she is going to beat up Nair. But Meiry is frightened of her because she
carries a razor. When she went to hit Nair she got it. Nair
tore off her clothes and left her naked. What laughter there
was! What a delicious spectacle for the *favelado* who pro-
foundly appreciates anything pornographic! The children
laughed and clapped their hands as if they were applauding
a puppet show. Afterward the kids divided into groups to
talk about it:

"I saw"

"I didn't see"

"I wanted to see"

Actually the children don't get excited any more when they
see a naked woman. They're used to it. The children think
that all women's bodies are alike. The only difference is in
the color. My boys ask me why a woman's body has this
or that. I pretend I don't understand the questions. They say:

"Mama is a dope. She doesn't know anything."

June 26   I heard the rumor that the police are going to
demand the *favelados* get off State land where they've built
their shacks without permission. Many people who had
houses here in the favela moved to State land because there,
when it rains, there's no mud. They say they're going to
build a children's playground. What I think is: ironic is that
the land once had brick houses on it and the State appropri-
ated it. Now John Doe is building his shack.

June 27   Today Leila is drunk. I've been asking myself how
a woman with two tender-age children can drink herself into
unconsciousness. Two men carried her home on their arms.
And if she rolls around in bed and crushes the just-born
child?

What I think is interesting is when a person enters a bar
or a saloon, very soon someone offers him a drink of *pinga*.
Why don't they offer a kilo of rice, beans, candy, etc. . . . ?

There are people here in the favela who say that I'm trying
to be a bigshot because I don't drink *pinga*. I am alone. I
have three children. If I got the alcohol habit, my sons will
not respect me. Even writing this I'm doing something
stupid. I don't have to explain myself to anyone. To con-
clude: I don't drink because I don't like it, and that ends it.
I prefer to put my money into books, rather than alcohol.
If you think that I'm acting correctly, I beg you to say:

"Very well, Carolina!"

June 28 Tonight we're going to have a race here in the favela. The race is sponsored by the Blacks and Reds. They bought *pinga* to make *quentão*.[18] *Quentão* for the adults and sweet potato candy for the children. They make a bonfire and put lights in the square. I'm waiting for the race to see who's going to win. For the winner the prize is a medal. A bottle of wine and candy for the second. The last one gets rotten eggs and a candle. The course is from the favela until the Pari Church. The only one who's really drunk is Valdemar. There's decorum in the favela today!

There are always a large number of children in the favela. One couple has eight children, another has six, and so on like that.

Senhor Alfredo gave a dance. He played the victrola. Only the *nordestinos* danced because the *Paulistas* are bored stiff, listening and dancing to *Pisa na Fulô*.[19] While the dance was on I used the time to get some water. I straightened up the kitchen and went back to the bonfire.

At ten to 9 they started the race. While waiting for the racers' return I visited. Dona Ida Cardoso watched over the fire. I said that in the center of the city they didn't build bonfires. A woman told me that in the city the bonfires are in another form. The racers came back. The first one was Joaquim. When it came time to award third-place prize, Armin, who was the judge, ran into difficulty because there were two men who said they had come in together. Then the women became judges. They made such a fuss that Armin ended up by awarding the prize to the one appointed by the boisterous women, who always have the final word. They served *quentão* and wine. I got happy. I danced with Senhor Binidito and with Armin. When I realized that the alcohol was confusing my senses I went to lie down. Before I laid down I gave João a beating because he is so badly behaved.

I forget to say that when I was warming by the fire, the women began talking that they had seen a picture of Zuza in the newspapers. They were pleased. I sensed that Senhor Zuza with that party he gave for the people in place of gaining friends he gained enemies.

I told Zuza that he would come out in the papers! I heard

18 *Quentão:* a drink of hot *pinga* sugarcane alcohol mixed with ginger.

19 *Pisa Na Fulô:* a popular northeastern song about dancing on a flower.

a man saying Zuza was a sharpie. But it was the curses of mothers who spent money and didn't get anything in return that stuck to him like glue.

June 29 At the church I got two kilos of macaroni, candy and crackers. I bought three sandwiches for the children. When I got back to the favela I met Senhor Aldo. The favela was organizing a race just for women. On "A" Street there was a dance. Now that the favela has become crowded with *nordestinos* there is more scheming. More squabbles and more distractions. The favela is always hot as a pepper. I stayed in the streets until 9 o'clock watching the goings-on to see how people act at night. I had already turned in when Florentina and Binidito started up. Florentina dying of hunger. She complained that her daughter Vilma hadn't won anything and having run in the race she deserved a medal. Who came in in first place was Iracema. Florentina is black. But she's so different from the other blacks because she's very ambitious. She schemes to profit from everything she does. I believe that if she owned a slaughterhouse people would have to eat the bones and the skins of the animals.

What squabbling there was in that women's race. Everybody wanted to win. I just stayed watching. I didn't interfere because I don't like squabbles. Dona Rosa who rents shacks here in the favela can skin you alive. She came to tell Senhor Francisco to give her 4,000 cruzeiros, that the time to pay the rent on the land was here.

"And this money that I've already given you can't be included in the sale of the shack?"

"No. It can't. That money only goes to pay the rent."

That was Dona Rosa's answer to Senhor Francisco. Poor Senhor Francisco. He is ill and on a pension and pays 700 a month for rent and 100 for electricity. He supports four people.

I am going to lie down. I think it must be 1 in the morning.

When I was resting I heard them saying that on "A" Street the *Baianos* were fighting. I went to see. What happened was that Sergio was holding a dance. And the *nortistas* were giving another. And were dancing with the door closed. And Chó's woman went to dance at the *nortistas'* party. But she only danced with the sharp ones and a *Pernambucano* invited her to dance with him. She didn't want to dance. She looked him over carefully and then said she didn't want to dance with him. The *Pernambucano*, when he saw he was refused, got furious. He pulled a knife out of his belt and went for Chó's woman. The only things I've ever seen move fast were rats, rabbits, and lightning. But Chó's woman, when she saw that knife coming in her direction, even outdid lightning. The people snatched the knife from him. The *Pernambucano* ran out snorting and shouting:

"Today I kill! Today blood will run in the favela."

He went running toward "B" Street, ripped a board out of the fence of Senhor Antonio Venancio, and returned to "A" Street. Arriving at Chó's house he shouted:

"Come on out! Come on out, you cheap tramp!"

Then there was tremendous confusion. All the *nortistas* spoke at once and I didn't understand anything. If they are like this in the North, then the North must be horrible.

In that confusion Chó's woman vanished like smoke.

Another thing I saw today—St. Peter's day. What I saw in the favela and is not right is this: there is a soldier here named Taubaté. He is the favorite of some women here in the favela. The soldier is dangerous. It would be a good thing if the lieutenant would remove this soldier from the favela. The slightest thing with him and he shoots. He's already wounded two in the favela.

On "C" Street, in the house of the late Senhor Sebastião Gonçalves, they made a bonfire. I got sleepy because I can't drink alcohol. And I drank *quentão*. The police from station 44 showed up. I followed them. As I've already explained, the *nortistas* talk so much that nobody understands anything. The police went away. I left "A" Street and went to "B" Street. I sat close to the fire. Everybody was talking. Their conversation didn't interest me but I stayed. They were talking about the fights. Of the soccer match in Switzerland and in the possibility of man going to the moon. Some said man would go. Others said he wouldn't go. And when I heard all that "will go" and "won't go" I started thinking there will be a fight because everything here in the favela that starts like that ends in a fight.

I was waiting for the Portuguese Sports Club to set off the fireworks, because if I went to bed before, I'd just wake up when they exploded. A woman who was feeding the fire said that Black Angelina beat her son Argemiro, who is eight, and doesn't want him to go to "A" Street to get water.

June 30 I made coffee and went to look for water. I heard

a scream and went to see what it was. It was Odete fighting
with her "companion." She said:

"Dona Carolina, go call the police!"

I told her she'd better calm down.

"Odete, you're pregnant!"

They were attracting attention. I've been in the favela
for 11 years and I still get sick witnessing these scenes. Odete
was half nude with her breasts hanging out.

They fight without knowing why they're fighting. The
neighbors told me that Odete threw boiling water in her
"companion's" face.

Today many men didn't go to work. It's a thing on Monday. They act as if they're already exhausted from over-
work before the week begins.

July 1 I've been thinking that if this diary is ever published, it's going to make a lot of people angry. Here are
people that, when they see me coming, go away from their
windows or close their doors. These things don't bother me.
In fact it pleases me because then I don't have to stop and
talk to them. When I went over to the factory I saw many
tomatoes. I was going to pick them up when the manager
came out. I didn't go near because he doesn't like people to
pick them up. When they unload the trucks, the tomatoes fall
on the ground, and when the trucks pull out, they squash
them. But human beings are like that. They prefer to see
things spoil than let others get some use from them. When
he went away I picked some up anyway. Afterward I went
looking for more paper. I met Samson, the mailman. He still
hasn't cut his hair. His eyes were red. I thought: has he been
crying? Or does he want to smoke or is he hungry? Such
common things here in Brazil. I stared at his faded uniform.
President Kubstchek who likes pomp should give his mail-
men other uniforms. He looked at me with my sack of
paper. I figured he trusted me. Helpless people, like the
mailman, get their spirits lifted when they meet someone
who sympathizes with them.

I don't like Kubstchek. A man that has a fancy name that
the people know how to say but nobody knows how to
spell.[20] The *Baiano* husband of Dora Zefa is my neighbor
and I heard him complaining about José Carlos annoying
him. All I know is that with so many *Baianos* in the favela,

[20] Here Carolina misspells it too.

the old-time *favelados* are moving out. They try to be superior by force. To be rid of them the *favelados* sacrifice, buy land, and pull out. I told him:

"Your children also annoy me. They open my cupboards and what they find they carry off."

"Oh, I didn't know this."

And he wouldn't have known either, because I don't make complaints against children. I like children.

A *nortista* named Dona Chiquinha lives here who is a seamstress. I liked her very much. I helped her in every way I could. One day my boy José Carlos was playing near her house and she threw water on him. The other day I met her, when a truck came to dump rotten pineapples in the favela, and I asked her why she had thrown water on my son.

"I threw cold water. But if he bothers me once more, I swear I'll throw hot water with soda to blind him, so he'll not annoy anyone else."

My friendship for Dona Chiquinha cooled off. The other day she came and asked me if I wanted a fight and if so she'd go and get a knife. I didn't give her the satisfaction.

July 3 I was writing when I heard my neighbor Antonio Nascimento scold José Carlos. Now he's strutting around, saying he's going to beat the boy. If he deserved it it would be one thing but he is picking on him. Where have you ever seen a 48-year-old man dare a child of nine years to fight? But Antonio Nascimento was born with twisted ideas.

Dirce's daughter died. They were twins. She had had double births before. Last year a pair of twins died. The boy one day, the girl the next. And now the other has withered away.

When someone dies here in the favela the sharpies go into the streets begging for money to bury the dead. They pocket the money and spend it on drink.

July 4 When I was walking down Eduardo Chaves Street, a woman called me, gave me some aluminum pans, paper, and a kilo of roasted beef with potatoes. I think she gave me the meat because of Vera, who told her one day that she would like to move her crib to the market and live there. Because there they had many good things to eat. And that she likes meat and wants to marry a butcher. I think of my daughter and get sick inside. She hates to live in the favela.

One day a black showed up in the favela and said her name was Vitoria. She came with a boy named Cezar. The black told me that she was the maid of Dona Mara, who danced at the Oasis Bar on 7 of April Street. She wanted me to loan her a book of poetry and I could go and get it any time I wanted it back. The Negress told me she was studying at the Conservatory of Drama and Music. It was Florentina who had pointed out my shack to her. She gave me this address: St. John Avenue 190, 82nd floor, apartment 23. What had me worried was that that building had 82 floors. I hadn't read that São Paulo had such a high building as yet. Afterward I thought: How can I who don't leave the garbage dump possibly know what's going on in the living room? With the insistence of Florentina I loaned her the book.

When I went into the city looking for number 190, I didn't find it. I went to the Oasis Bar looking for Dona Mara to know how I could locate her maid. They told me that Dona Mara frequented the bar but that she usually arrived about 1 in the morning. I left a note for Dona Mara and never got an answer. But the day that I run into that nigger Vitoria, she's going to be sorry.

I soaped the clothes. Then I went to finish washing them in the lagoon. The State Health Department has said that the water of the lagoon transmits a snail's disease. They come and tell us what we try to ignore. They leave us with the polluted lagoon and do nothing about supplying us with good water.

Dona Alice is unhappy because she rented a shack from Dona Rosa who now wants to sell the shack. She wants 4,000 cruzeiros. And Alice's husband has got the money but won't buy it. Now Dona Rosa won't speak to either of them.

I've never seen a person as ambitious as she is. If it were only ambition, but it's really shaded jealousy. When I won my red skirt she was furious. She said:

"I was the only one who didn't win anything."

Now she built another shack and rented the one she was living in. Senhor Francisco is living there now.

When my children were smaller I used to lock them in when I went to pick up paper. One day I came home to find João crying. He told me:

"Mama, Dona Rosa threw dog shit in my face."

I made a fire, heated water and washed the children. I was terrified with the evilness of Dona Rosa. She knows that here in the favela no one is allowed to rent a shack. But she rents. She is the worst woman I've ever seen in my life. Why is it that the poor don't have pity on the other poor?

July 5   Brother Luiz visited us today in the church car. He told us he's going to teach catechism to the children so they can make their first communion. Saturday he's going to teach us the biblical texts.

July 6   I woke up at 4:30 because of Neide's cough. I knew that cough wouldn't let me sleep. I got up and gave her a little syrup because I felt sorry for her. She doesn't have any father. When the father was sick, the mother left them. There are three girls. Neide's mother has a heart of stone. She wouldn't take care of her sick husband nor raise her children, who are cared for by their grandparents.

I heated rice and the fish and fed the children. Afterward I went to pick up kindling wood. It seems that I came into the world predestined to pick things up. The only thing I don't pick up is happiness.

I spread the clothes out to dry. Beside me was the wife of the *nortista* who slept with Chó's woman. She was nervous and talked a lot. Seemed as if she had an electric tongue. Seemed like Carlos Lacerda when he talked about Getulio. She said she washed the clothes of Chó's woman. And her own husband paid her to do it.

It's 5:30. Brother Luiz is coming to show a film here in the favela. He's already put up the screen and the *favelados* are waiting.

The people in the brick houses near the favela say they don't know why people of culture pay attention to the people of the favela. The kids of the favela complained when the movie began showing scenes of the Bible and the Birth of Christ. Brother Luiz arrived in the church car. He is a priest who helps the *favelados*. While the movie played the Brother explained. When the three wise men came on the Brother explained they were wise because they could read the future of people from the stars. He asked if anyone knows the name of one of them. One was very well known and called Baltazar.

"And the other is called Pelé," [21] shouted a little black.

Everybody laughed. A truck arrived with the soccer team at the moment the padre was praying. My kids came home from the movie and I gave them supper. Vera was happy

---

[21] Pelé: Brazil's world-famed soccer star.

and told all the bad things that José Carlos had done. João lost the 11 cruzeiros I gave him to go to the Rialto Cinema. He put the money in a wallet and went with some boys of the favela. One of them already knows how to steal wallets.

July 7 I went to Dona Juana and she gave me some bread. I passed by the factory to see if there were any tomatoes. There was a lot of kindling wood. I was just about to pick up some pieces when I heard a black man tell me that I wasn't to mess with that wood or he would hit me. I told him to go ahead and hit because I wasn't afraid. He was putting this wood into a truck. He looked at me scornfully and said:

"Nut!"

"And it's just because I am crazy that you'd better not mess with me. I've got all the vices. I rob and I fight and I drink. I spend 15 days at home and 15 days in jail."

He made a move toward me and I told him:

"I am from the favela of Canindé. I know how to cut with a *gilette* and a razor and I'm learning to handle a fish knife. A *nortista* is giving me lessons. If you want to hit me go ahead."

I started to search my pockets.

"Where's my razor? Today you're going to walk around with only one ear. When I drink a few *pingas* I go half crazy. It's that way in the favela, anybody who shows up there we beat them, steal their money and everything they have in their pockets."

The black kept quiet. I went away. When someone insults us, all we have to do is tell what the favela is. They leave us in peace. We of the favela are feared. I dared the black because I knew he would go away. I don't like to fight.

When I was returning I met Nelson da Vila Guilherme. He said something I didn't like. I pretended I didn't understand what he said.

"But you with all your intelligence, you don't understand why I'm following you around?"

When I got back to the favela my children were not there. I called. None of them appeared. I went to Senhor Eduardo and bought a half liter of oil and 16 cruzeiros of sausage. I found the 46 cruzeiros that João received when he sold the scrap iron. 46 with my 20 gave me 66. On my return I kept watching the favela men. Most of them don't work on Monday. I went to Manuel and met João who was just coming back. He said he found some cans and got four cruzeiros. I asked him about Vera. He told me he left her at home. And she was with José Carlos.

Then I heard Vera's voice. She said:

"José Carlos. Here's Mama!"

They came running toward me. She said that she and José Carlos had gone out begging. He had one of my sacks on his back. I walked ahead of them so they wouldn't see my smile but told him he should be studying his lessons. I had to go into the city.

While I was dressing I heard the voice of Durvalino arguing with a strange drunk. Women started to appear. They never miss these things. They can stand hours and hours just watching. They don't think of anything even if they left a pot on the stove. A fight for them is just as important as the bullfights in Madrid are for the Spanish. I saw Durvalino strike the drunk and try to strangle him. The drunk had no force to fight back. Armin and some others took Durvalino's hands off the drunk's neck and carried him to the other side of the river. And Durvalino stayed bragging about what he had done.

I went to register to vote. When I got to Semanario Street, I needed a photo for registration papers. I had a picture taken in Foto Lara. It cost me 60 cruzeiros. While I waited for the photographs I talked to the people there. They were all pleasant. I got my pictures and went to stand in the line. I talked with a woman whose husband works in the mayor's office. She wanted to know who I was going to vote for. I told her I was going to vote for Dr. Adhemar. I left the Board Room and took the streetcar. When I got off at the last stop I went to the butcher to buy hamburger. I bought a half kilo of rice. I asked the woman selling newspapers if she was going to vote. I was thinking of my children who must be hungry. Vera started asking for something to eat. I heated it and gave it. João ate and so did José Carlos. They told me about Dona Aparecida's brother-in-law who went to the First Aid Station. He had been run over and was in a cast.

When I go into the city I have the impression that I'm in paradise. I think it just wonderful to see all the women and children so well dressed. So different from the favela. The different-colored houses with their vases of flowers. These views enchant the eyes of the visitors to São Paulo who never know that the most famous city in South America is ill with ulcers—the favelas.

July 8   I wasn't feeling well and went to bed early. I awoke because of the clamor in the street. I couldn't understand what they were saying because everyone was talking at the same time and there were many voices. All sorts of voices. I wanted to get up and ask them if they would mind letting people sleep. But I know I'd be wasting my time. All of them were drunk. Leila was giving her show. And their shouts didn't let the neighbors sleep. At 4 o'clock I began to write. When I wake up it's difficult to go back to sleep. I started thinking of this troubled life and of the words Brother Luiz gave us in his humble sermons. I thought: if Brother Luiz was married, had children, and earned the minimum wage, I would like to see if he would be so humble. He said that God blesses only those who suffer with resignation. If the Brother saw his children eating rotten food already attacked by vultures and rats, he would stop talking about resignation and rebel, because rebellion comes from bitterness.

I sent João to buy ten cruzeiros of cheese. He met Adalberto and told him to come and talk to me. That I had found some boards and was going to make a little room where I could write and keep my books. I went out in search of paper. There is little paper in the streets because that other poor soul is also picking it up. He sells paper, buys *pinga*, and drinks. Afterward he sits down and weeps silently. I was so sleepy that I couldn't even walk. Dona Anita gave me some candy but my paper only brought me 23 cruzeiros. When I got back to the favela João was reading a comic book. I warmed up the food and fed them. That noise at night that I heard: the women were gossiping that the men drank 14 liters of *pinga*. And Leila insulted a young man, and he beat her. They threw her on the ground and kicked her in the face. An act of the jungle. But when Leila drinks she annoys people. She even bothered Chiclet, a good Negro who lives here in the favela. He didn't want to touch her but she degraded him so much that he hit her with such force he broke off two teeth. That's why everybody now calls him "The Dentist." Leila's face swelled up so bad she had to take penicillin. Today is the day of the wailers. There is a *nortista* who lives here that when she drinks, burns up your patience. Her son took a lover. A woman who could be his grandmother. The future wife came to live with his mother.

When the old lady drinks she gets nasty and argues. She never gave them any peace. So, he ran away with the woman. Now the old lady is wailing. She wants her son back.

It's 5 o'clock. José Carlos arrived. I'm going to change his clothes and take him to Gouveia's Store and buy him a pair of shoes. At Gouveia's he picked out his shoes. 159 cruzeiros. Senhor Gouveia let me have them for 150. José is happy. He watches people as they go by to see if they are noticing his new shoes.

When I got back to the favela I met Senhor Francisco. He loaned me his wagon and I went to look for boards. I put Vera inside the wagon. And José Carlos and Ninho came too. Going, it was easy. The wagon sped over the concrete as if it were automatic. I found all kinds of wood. I piled it it in front and in back. I figured I'd have to carry it in two loads. What I have to do, I do. Without even thinking of the work involved. At the corner of Araguaia and Canindé there is a lot of mud and I ran into trouble because I was bare-foot and my feet slipped in the mud. There was no way I could solidly plant them. I fell. A man appeared and pulled the wagon for me. He told me to steady the pile of wood. I thanked him and went on. Going over the streetcar tracks the boards fell off the wagon. José Carlos appeared, saw my troubles, and said:

"Why don't you rest? Now you have a man to help you." I gave thanks to God when I finally got back to the favela. There was a woman waiting for me. She told me that João had hurt her daughter. She said that my son had tried to rape her two-year-old daughter and that she was going to tell everything to the Judge. If he did this, then the person who should lock him up is I. I wept.

I put José Carlos to bed and went out with João. I went to the court to see if there was a possibility they might lock him up. I had to take him out of the streets because now anything that goes wrong they'll say he did it. At the court a nice gentleman who was on duty told me to come back on the tenth because the ninth was a holiday. I left the court and took a streetcar because it was cheaper. At the end of the line João stood in the doorway of a bakery shop and I sat down to rest a little. When I returned to the favela it was midnight. I was upset.

July 9 I had nightmares. I am so nervous that if I had

wings I would fly to the desert or the jungle. There are times when I am furious with myself for letting men trick me into having these children.

When I was getting ready to go out Dona Alice came to tell me that two boys from the State Children's Shelter were hiding in the favela. I went to see. They were in yellow uniforms. No shoes and no shirt. Just a jacket over the skin. They were lost. I asked if they wanted some coffee. They said no.

I went back inside and got ready to go into the streets. José Carlos stayed with the boys. He came and asked me if I could arrange some clothes for the boys.

"Go, call them!"

He went out and came back with the boys. One was a light-skinned mulatto with an ugly face and a Negro nose. The other was a pretty white. They told me the horrors of the shelters. That not only children without parents to care for them were sent there, but young criminals who were sentenced by the court as well. All thrown together and with no special consideration for the innocent ones. They went hungry, cold, and were constantly beaten. They asked me if I could get them some shirts. I gave them shirts and trousers. I asked them their names. The mulatto was Antonio and the white was Nelson. I asked if they knew how to read. They said yes. I gave them some coffee. They said they lived in Vila Maria favela and that they each had mothers. They advised my sons to be good to me. That sons are better off with their mothers. That the best thing in the world is a mother. They put on the clothes I gave them. Nelson's trousers had so many patches they must have weighed three kilos. When they left they looked at the number of my shack and begged me not to let them intern João there, that the food was terrible. They were forced to wash dishes and if a child threw the rest of his dinner in the garbage they made him pick it out and eat it.

My sons were horrified with the narration of the two fugitives. I decided not to intern João because he has an appetite. I saw how they wanted to get rid of those yellow clothes.

The boys asked my name and gave me big smiles. I thought: why is it that the boys who run away from the shelter come complaining about the organization? I felt that in the State Shelter the children's morals were lowered. The

Judges don't have the ability to shape the character of the children. What's lacking? Concern for the unfortunate or money from the State?

In 1952 I tried to get into Vera Cruz hospital and went to the minors' court to talk to Dr. Nascimento if there was a possibility to intern my children. He told me that if my children entered the shelter they would come out criminals.

I was horrified hearing a Judge say that.

When the late-lamented Itaboca Street still existed, I say lamented because there are so many men lamenting the closing of that whorehouse, I went there and saw the sordid women and I asked them:

"Where were you raised?"

"In the Children's Shelter."

"Do you know how to read?"

"No! Why? Are you a priest?"

I stopped the questioning. They didn't know how to read, nor even take care of a home. The only thing that they knew so well that they could lecture and give out diplomas was pornography.

Poor orphans of the Court!

I went to pick up paper. I didn't feel well. The people in the street know when I'm unhappy. I got 36 cruzeiros. I went back. I didn't talk to anyone. There is no meaning to my life. I began to think that my insipid life was too long. Today the sun didn't come out. The day is as sad as my soul. I left João locked up inside studying. I told him that a man who goes wrong is vaccinated by public opinion. And from what I've seen, those who live in the favela can't hope for anything good to come out of the surroundings. It is the adults who contribute to the delinquency of the minors. We have our professors of scandals: Leila, Meiry, Zefa, Pitita, and Deolinda.

When I returned to the favela I found a *nortista* with a knife in his hand hunting for my boy. When he saw me he didn't say anything. But *I* talked to *him*.

I heard the women at the junk yard saying that Senhor João on Porto Street died and has been waiting two days for money to be buried. I started out to see him. But I began to feel ill and decided to lie down for a while. It's been two years since I've laid down during the day. I thought of Senhor João who had been ill for a long time. Paralyzed. He said he wanted to die because he couldn't stand being supported by his wife. Life, even without illness, is difficult to lead. His wife, Dona Angelina, worked for the two of them. She got some help from the Vincent Fathers, but she was always scheming against them, and they stopped helping her.

I slept a little. Afterward I started to write. Dona Alice gave me a bowl of soup. The day I leave the favela I'm going to light a candle for St. Sebastian. I heard Deolinda fighting with her husband.

They were living together and the Vincents advised them to marry. He drinks a lot and she can double it. She says her stomach won't accept coffee in the morning. When she drinks it she vomits. So in the morning she drinks *pinga* and spends the rest of the day sucking her thumb. It's disgusting to see a woman of 50 years sucking her thumb. The mother-in-law also drinks. They make up the most scandalous trio on "C" Street.

I'm keeping the clothes of the boys from the Children's Shelter as a proof. I'm horrified with the odor of sweat. Pure neglect!

July 10 I left my bed at five in the morning to get water. I don't like to be with those women because at the spigot they speak of everybody and everything. I feel so bad. If I could only lie down for a while! But I don't have anything for the children to eat. The only thing to do is go out. I left João studying. I only got ten cruzeiros and found some metal. I found a wood drill and a schoolboy asked for it. I sold it to him. He gave me three cruzeiros for a cup of coffee. I went by the street market. I bought a sweet potato and a fish. When I got back to the favela it was noon. I heated food for João and cleaned up the shack. Later I sold some tin cans and got 40 cruzeiros. I came back to the favela and made supper.

Deolinda and her husband were taken away in a patrol car. Probably they've been arrested.

The afternoon went by slowly. The Believers are coming with their musical instruments and praising God. Here in the favela there is a shack on "B" Street where the Believers come to pray three times a week. Part of the shack is covered with tin and the rest in tile. There was a day when they were praying and the bums of the favela threw rocks on the shack and broke the tile. Those that hit the tin made a loud noise. Even being insulted they don't give up. They ask the *favelados* not to rob, drink, and to love your neighbor as yourself. The Believers don't permit women to attend their services who are wearing slacks or low-cut dresses. The *favelados* scorn their advice.

I went to get a can full of water and a woman was complaining:

"If I was young I wouldn't live in this favela, not one day. But now I'm old. The old don't get their own way."

Here in this favela you see things that make your hair stand on end. A favela is a strange city and the mayor here is the Devil. The drunks who are hidden during the day come out at night to bother you.

I can see that of all the people who live in the favela not one of them likes the place.

July 11 I got out of bed at 5:30. I was tired from writing and sleepy. But here in the favela you can't sleep, because the shacks are humid and Neide coughs a lot and keeps me awake. I went to get water and the line was enormous. What an unpleasant thing to wait at that spigot. There's always a fight or someone who wants to know all about the private life of another. In the morning the area around the spigot is covered with shit. I am the one who cleans it up. Because the others aren't interested.

When I got back to the favela I was ill and had a pain in my legs. My sickness is physical as well as moral.

July 12 I went to the slaughterhouse and got a few bones. I'm ill. I bought two sweet rolls for João and Vera. I found some tomatoes. I met an educated and well-speaking black who told me he lived in Jaçanã. I wanted to ask him his name but I was embarrassed. He gave two cruzeiros to João and I bought some kerosene. I went home, then went to Senhor Manuel to sell some scrap iron. The junk yard was closed. I went back home and laid down. I was cold and upset inside. The people of the favela know that I'm ill. But nobody shows up here to help me out. I didn't let João go out and he spent the entire day reading. He talks to me and I tell him of the unfortunate things that exist in the world. My son now knows what the world is; between us the language of children has ended.

José Carlos went to the street market. I boiled the bones to make soup. Vera didn't want any. Brother Luiz is putting up the screen to show a movie. I'm not going to go because I'm sick. João asked me to go. I told him that as long as we continue to live in the favela he was not to play with anybody. I don't want another incident like the first one. Before

I used to speak and he would get angry. Now I speak and he listens. I'm going to tell my son about the really serious things in life only when he comes of age.

My son, at 11 years, had already wanted a woman. I explained to him that he must graduate from school, then study even more because a primary school education is not really very much.

July 13 The nurses are coming with Brother Luiz, they are going to cure the sores of the *favelados*. They are teaching the children to pray. I'd like to know how Brother Luiz discovered that the *favelados* have physical sores.

I heated a supper for the children. I heard Meiry inviting Nair to a dance over on "A" Street. Vera is coughing. I got up and gave her a pill. I have a fever. I can't raise myself up. I'm waiting for José Carlos to come back. When he came he gave me the box that I keep my medicines in and I took an aspirin and the pain started going away and I fell asleep. I woke up at 2 in the morning with Arnaldo and Leila fighting.

July 14 I spent the day in bed because I have a fever and a pain in my legs. I don't have any money but I left some scrap with Senhor Manuel and I sent José Carlos to get it weighed and to collect for it. I got 22 cruzeiros. I spent five of it on bread, five more of it on sugar and a pill. I got up only to get lunch ready, and went back to bed. José Carlos heard Florentina telling that she thought I was crazy, because I write and don't get anything for it.

July 15 Today is the birthday of my daughter Vera Eunice. I can't give her a party for this would be just like trying to grab ahold of the sun with my hands. Today there's not going to be any lunch. Only supper.

I'm feeling worse. Yesterday I prayed to be cured. Thank God the saints are still protecting me. Because there is no extra money for me to go see a doctor.

I went out to pick up paper and took my children with me. Now I want to have João where I can keep my eyes on him. I went to Senhor Manuel and sold some scrap. I got 25 cruzeiros. I bought bread. When I returned to the favela there was a Portuguese selling cows' intestines. I bought half a kilo of stomach. But I don't like to deal with Portuguese. They have no education. They are obscene, pornographic, and stupid. When they bargain with a black they think they can cheat her. They think they're more intelligent than anybody else. The Portuguese told Fernanda that he would give her a piece of liver if she would let him . . . her. She didn't want to. There are blacks that don't like whites. She walked away without buying. He couldn't sell because he was so insolent.

July 16 There was no paper in the streets. I went past the slaughterhouse. They had thrown a lot of sausage in the garbage. I sorted out the ones that were not rotten. I don't want to grow weak and I can't afford to buy. I have an appetite like a lion. So, I have to go through garbage.

July 17 Leila and Arnaldo fought all night. They didn't let us sleep. I got out of bed at 5:30 and carried water. At the spigot there's always a row.

"You went in front of me!"

"I did not!"

And so it goes. One day Dona Silvia's husband Antonio was at the spigot and arguing, he and a *nortista,* Manoel, father of Zé Maria. While they were trading insults, I arrived. The *nortista* took out his knife. Antonio is 65 years old, but when he saw that knife, he gave a jump equal to Ademar Ferreira doing the triple jump in the Olympics.

I went to look for paper. I got 60 cruzeiros. I stopped to talk with Dona Anita. She is worried about the news of war. A war is thankless for the young. The life of a private is bitter. The heroes are the soccer players. The Privates are chased by evil women. And those Privates are our sons.

I've heard it said that General Teixeira Lott, Minister of War, is not going to send troops to the Middle East. If that's true then I think we should look upon our general with new respect for he has shown his devotion for the people and the country.

July 18 I went out to look for paper. I heard women complaining with tears in their eyes that they couldn't bear the rising cost of living any more. I took João with me to avoid any trouble. I went by the newsstand on Avenue Tiradentes and stopped to talk with the vendor and some men.

When I got back to the favela it was 12:30. Durvalino came by with a piece of meat in his hand. He stopped to play with Neide and started to talk foolishness to me. He is worthless and would make a terrible husband. He gave the piece of meat to Dona Aparecida.

July 19 I went to the bakery. The owner told me he wasn't going to give away any more crackers. I came back picking up everything that I found along the way. It's raining and I didn't want to look for paper. When I got back in the favela Vera told me that a *Baiana* had insulted her. A woman of 32 years old fighting with a child of five! A neighbor who saw the *Baiana* threatening Vera confirmed it. As soon as that creature sees me she starts insulting me. She brandished a knife at José Carlos and said was going to stick him with it.

I sold some scrap to Senhor Manuel. I got 55 cruzeiros. I took very little scrap with me and thought that was a lot of money. I asked Senhor Manuel if he hadn't made a mistake.

I went to the market, bought one kilo of beans and one of kidney. Everything else I picked up from the ground. When a Portuguese threw some lettuce leaves on the ground and I picked them up he shouted:

"The customer from the society columns is here!"

I'm not going to wash clothes today because I don't have money to buy soap. I'm going to read and write.

Leila grabbed a hatchet and chopped the bottom of the washtub. The tub belongs to Ivone Horacio who cut me five times with a razor in 1952.

The hearing was canceled because she didn't show up at court. She chopped a hole in the bottom. I was horrified and saddened.

Two *nortistas* were fighting. They go around looking for insults. Victor Frankenstein, a bully, was grabbed by Valdemar Espadela. Everybody was for this because Victor wants to be the Lampeão of the favela. There were just two blows. Now the women are saying that they are going to take up a collection and buy a wool shirt for Valdemar to commemorate his good deed.

July 20   I was writing when I heard the voice of Senhor Binidito. I asked him to come in. He introduced a man from the Divine Master Spirit Center, who had come to give cards to people who were looking for warm clothes for children. They were to be given on the 23rd. I was so pleased that I got out of bed fast. I explained to the gentlemen what I was writing.

I started to write again when Adalberto arrived. He is going to make a fence for me. To keep out those *nortistas* who come over here for any reason to bother me. Those who worked on the fence were Adalberto and Luiz, a recent guest in the favela, and Dona Rosa's José. They bought *pinga* and I mixed it with sugar and lemon juice. I gave them lunch. It was 1 o'clock when I started to write again. Senhor Alexandre began to beat his wife. Dona Rosa intervened. He kicked the children. When he started to strangle Dona Nena, Dona Rosa called for help. Then a soldier, Edison Fernandes, went to ask Senhor Alexandre not to beat his wife. He didn't pay any attention and threatened the soldier with a knife. Edison Fernandes gave him a few fast hard ones. Alexandre flew like a balloon tossed in the wind.

The soldier Edison asked me to telephone the police. I went fast. I telephoned and ran back. When I got to the favela the fight was hot. Alexandre was threatening the children who had come to watch and he started for my son João. He was shouting insults at Edison, wanting to hit him in the face:

"I'll give my wife to you! A woman after she gets married is supposed to support her husband! I don't permit soldiers to come into my house. Are you interested in my wife?"

When the *favelados* saw me they shouted:

"Where are the police?"

"I just called them."

In five minutes the patrol car arrived. Vera and I got into the car. Vera started to smile thinking it was delicious to ride in an automobile. When the people from the brick house saw me inside the car they shouted:

"Crime in the favela!"

And ran in the directon of the favela.

José Carlos came back from the movies and I told him all about the show that Alexandre gave. He said that Alexandre was at the streetcar stop. I didn't believe it. Was it possible that the police would let loose such a dangerous man who didn't even respect children?

Being as I had been warned, I wasn't startled when I heard Alexandre arguing with Edison, the soldier's mother. I intervened because she's pregnant. I went looking for Bobo so he would take Alexandre out of the house. But Binidito shoved Alexandre outside. He went into his shack and shut the door. He was so drunk that he couldn't even stand.

We lay down. I was upset because I wanted to spend the day writing. I couldn't sleep. I was exhausted from running so much when I went to call the police. I woke up at 4 in the morning with the voice of Alexandre mistreating his wife again and cursing the soldier Edison. He said:

"That dirty nigger hit me! But he'll pay for it! I'll get even!"

Seeing that Alexandre wasn't going to stop I went to the police station. The officer on duty said:

"That favela is too much!"

He told me that if Alexandre continued bothering people, I should come back at 6 o'clock. I returned to the favela; he was in the street shouting insults. I decided to make coffee. I opened the window and threw a little water on Alexandre.

"You called the police on me! Stinking nigger! But you'll pay for it!"

July 21   I went out to pick up paper. I was still shocked over the scene Alexandre had played at dawn. I found a lot of scrap and a little paper. When I was near the newsstand I slipped and fell. Because I was very dirty a man cried out:

"Hunger!"

And he gave me some money. But I fell because I was sleepy.

I thought about Alexandre and why he never even thinks about working: because he forces his wife to beg. He has one child: Dica. The girl is nine years old. She begs for money in the morning and goes to school in the afternoon. The child knows the letters and the numbers, but she doesn't know how to make words. When she writes she puts down whatever letter comes into her head. She mixes numbers with letters. She writes like this:

ACR85CZbo4Up7Mno10E20

And it's almost two years since she started going to school.

When I was in the street Alexandre hit the mother of Edison the soldier. When I arrived he started to insult me:

"Dirty nigger. Common. Tramp. Garbage."

I don't have any patience; I cursed him and threw an empty glass in his face. He shut the window. He opened it again and I threw a scrub brush at him. He shut the window. Later on he opened it and started to insult Edison the soldier. Edison the soldier went to talk to him. When he saw the soldier he got frightened and said:

"That punch you gave me; you're going to pay for it."

Edison the soldier said to him:

"Then let's get this over with right now."

The children gathered around to look at the kind of scenes that I don't approve of. An improper spectacle. While the soldier argued with Alexandre I went to get some stones.

Edison the soldier gave him a punch in the face. And the children gave a cheer.

Alexandre became afraid of the soldier, went inside, and shut the door. He turned off the light and didn't make a sound all night.

July 22 I went out to work and told my neighbors:

"If Alexandre makes trouble, let me know."

I walked thinking of my wretched life. For two weeks I haven't been able to wash clothes for lack of soap. The beds are so filthy it makes me want to vomit.

I don't get upset when I see a stranger looking at my dirt. I think I'll start traveling through the streets with a sign on my back:

"If I'm dirty it's because I don't have soap."

I arrived at the slaughterhouse. The boys went inside and each one got a small sausage. While I was waiting a Spaniard came out to clean and he started shouting at me. Today I'm nervous and I'm not going to let a stranger shout at me.

There is a Spanish woman who comes to the slaughterhouse to pick meat from the garbage and when she saw the Spaniard she said:

"He isn't from my country. That's a Portuguese!"

And there was a Portuguese woman who said:

"That beast isn't from Portugal!"

And I, giving the final touch, said:

"Well, thank God, at least he's not a Brazilian!"

July 23 I left the bed at 7 o'clock. I was not well. Thank God Alexandre quieted down.

I warmed up some food for the children and started getting them ready to go to the Divine Master Center to get those free clothes. When the people saw the favela women in the streets they asked if we were on our way to the Ministry to present our manifesto.

"There has been a disagreement," I replied.

And the women laughed.

At the Divine Master Center, Senhor Pinheiro received us, smiling. There was no prejudice or class distinction. I got two light jackets, one for Vera and the other for José Carlos. João got a pullover sweater. Senhor Pinheiro's words cheered me up.

July 24 How horrible it is to get up in the morning and not have anything to eat. I even thought of suicide. But I am

~~killing myself now, by lack of food in the stomach.~~ And un-
~~happily I get up in the morning hungry.~~

The boys got a few hard rolls but they were covered with
cockroach droppings. I threw them away and we just drank
coffee. I put the last of the beans on to cook. I picked up
my sack and went out taking the children with me. I went to
see Dona Guilhermina, on Carlos de Campos Street. I asked
her for a little rice. She gave me rice and macaroni. I stayed
on to talk with her husband. He gave me some bottles to
sell. And I picked up some scrap metal.

After getting a few things for the children to eat, I felt
better. It calmed my spirit. I went to Senhor Manuel to sell
the bottles. I got 22 cruzeiros. I spent ten on bread and a cup
of coffee.

Returning to the favela, I made lunch and went to wash
clothes. Three weeks without washing clothes for lack of
soap. The neighbors were scandalized seeing the amount of
clothes that I washed. Dona Geralda, wife of João the
Portuguese, came looking for Fernanda saying that she had
robbed her washtub. She had even ransacked the house of
Fernanda's mother. Fernanda took Geralda back to her own
house and there they found the tub in the kitchen. She begged
Fernanda to forgive her and gave her a bottle of *pinga*. When
she received the bottle of *pinga* she was so pleased. She
smiled at the bottle and came praising Dona Geralda.

"What a good woman!"

Fernanda's anger disappeared when the *pinga* came in as
referee.

July 25   I found the day beautiful and happy. I went out
looking for paper.

July 26   I was dizzy with hunger because I got up very early.
I made more coffee. Later I went to wash clothes in the
lagoon, thinking of the State Health Department who published in the paper that here in the favela of Canindé there
are 160 positive cases of snail disease. But they don't give
any medicine to the *favelados*. The woman who ran a film
explaining the snail disease told us that the disease is very
difficult to cure. I didn't take the examination because I can't
buy the medicine to cure it.

I sent João to Senhor Manuel to sell some scrap. And I
went looking for paper. In the garbage at the slaughterhouse
there were many sausages. I picked out the best ones to make
soup. I went up and down the streets looking for scrap metal.

When I got to the streetcar stop I met José Carlos coming from the street market where he had been picking up vegetables.

Adalberto came looking for clothes. I didn't pay attention to him because he is becoming too familiar. Yesterday he talked dirty while Vera was near. He's annoying me.

Senhor Manuel arrived. He gave me 80 cruzeiros and I didn't want to take it. I was happy when I saw Senhor Manuel. I told him that I was going to spend all night writing. When he was leaving he said:

"It can be another day."

Our eyes met. I told him:

"See that you don't come back here. I'm an old woman. I don't want men. I only want my children."

He went away. He is very kind and educated. And pretty. Any woman would like to have a man as pretty as he is. Pleasant to talk to.

Brother Luiz came by and gave a catechism lesson to the children. Then they had a procession. I didn't go.

July 27 I heated food for the children and started to write. I looked for a place where I could write in peace. But here in the favela there aren't any such places. In the sun I feel the heat. In the shade I feel cold. I was wandering around with the notebooks in my hand when I heard angry voices. I went to see what it was. I thought it was a fight. I saw all the John Does running. A fight is a show that they don't miss. I'm so used to seeing fights that I'm not impressed. Someone had tossed fire into the automobile of Senhor Mario Pelasi. It burnt his soccer shoes, his socks, and the car seatcovers. Some boys saw the smoke in the car and went to tell him. He was playing soccer.

July 28 I left João and just took Vera and José Carlos. I was so unhappy! With a tremendous desire to kill myself. Today whoever is born and can put up with this life until death must be considered a hero. A current verse around is this one:

> I hear people saying
> Adhemar has a lot of money.
> Hasn't one got the right to be rich
> When he is a national, when he is a Brazilian?

Okay, let's leave Dr. Adhemar in peace because he has an

easy life. He's never hungry. He doesn't eat out of garbage cans like the poor. Once when I went to Dr. Adhemar's residence I met a man who gave me his card: Edson Marreira Branco.

He was so well dressed that he attracted all eyes. He told me that he wanted to get into politics. I asked him:

"What are your political plans?"

"I want to get as rich as Adhemar."

I was shocked. Nobody any more has any patriotism.

When I went by the slaughterhouse I met Dona Maria de José Bento who told me:

"If I don't start picking up things in the street, I'm going to go crazy. Only God has pity on us poor."

I showed her how to look for wild garlic. And I picked up a little coal. I said good-by to Dona Maria and went on. I met Dona Nené, director of a city school and João's teacher. I told her that I was very nervous and that there were times when I thought of killing myself. She told me that I should be calmer. I told her that there are days when I have nothing to give my children to eat.

July 30 I got 15 cruzeiros and went by the shoemaker to see if Vera's shoes were ready, because she complains when she has to go barefoot. They were, and she put on the shoes and began to smile. I stood watching my daughter's smile, because I myself don't know how to smile.

I met Rosalina who was arguing with Helio. He doesn't want it told that he and Olga have to beg. Rosalina said that she is alone and supports three children. She doesn't know that her son Celso is telling everybody that he is going to run away from home because he hates her. He thinks his mother is crude and stingy. He said he wants to be my son. Then I told him:

"If you were my boy you would be black. And being Rosalina's boy you are white."

He answered me:

"But if I was your son I wouldn't go hungry. Mama gets some hard bread and forces us to eat nothing but hard bread until it's all gone."

I started thinking about the unfortunate children who, even being tiny, complain about their condition in the world. They say that Princess Margaret of England doesn't like being a Princess. Those are the breaks in life.

July 31 I lit the fire and went to look for water. I sent José

Carlos for six cruzeiros worth of sugar. Luiz, who made the fence for me, came in and sat down. I told him that I was going out and when I went I preferred to leave my children by themselves.

I hurried out looking for paper. There was little paper in the streets. I'm getting sick of picking up paper, because when I get to the junk yard there is a woman named Cecilia who works there and she is a bitch. She insults me and I pretend I don't hear. She says I stink. On the 27th Cecilia didn't let José Carlos use the toilet shed. She is such a bitch that her presence even keeps the junk yard owner away.

Today I'm not nervous. I'm sad. Because I think things will turn out one way and they turn out the other. Antonio Nascimento, who lived here in the favela, moved. He and his "companion" were not happy here. Nobody wanted them in the favela. Because he ran out on four children and she on three children. Seven children suffering because of their parents. What did she gain by leaving her husband and children? She left a man with shoes to go with one who is barefoot.

August 1 The Welfare Department is arriving. They are coming to investigate the Portuguese who sells candy. On the 28th of July I went to visit him. He wanted some help. They claimed he didn't pay social security and they didn't come. He was moaning and had two Portuguese women visiting him. I asked him if he was better. He told me no. One of the women asked me:

"And what do you do?"

"I pick up paper, scrap iron, and in my free time I write."

She told me, with the wisest-sounding voice I ever heard:

"You must take care of your life!"

August 2 I dressed the boys and sent them to school. I went out and wandered around trying to get some money. I passed the slaughterhouse, picked up a few bones. Some women were pawing through the garbage looking for edible meat. They claimed it was only for dogs.

That's what I say—it's only for dogs. . . .

August 3 Today the children are only going to get hard bread and beans with *farinha* to eat. I'm so tired that I can't even stand up. I'm cold. Thank God we're not starving. Today He is helping me. I'm confused and don't know what to do. I'm walking from one side to the other because I can't stand being in a shack as bare as this. A house that doesn't have a fire in the stove is so sad! And pots boiling on the fire also serve as decoration. It beautifies a place.

I went to Dona Nené. She was in the kitchen. What a marvelous sight! She was cooking chicken, meat, and macaroni. She grated *half* a cheese to put on the macaroni!

She gave me some polenta with chicken. It's been ten years. . . . I almost didn't know what it was.

The smell of food in Dona Nené's house was so pleasant that tears streamed out of my eyes, because I felt so sorry for my children. They would have loved those delicacies.

When I returned to the favela Leila and Arnaldo were giving one of their shows. And the children were enjoying it.

I was writing when Vera came to tell me that they were handing out cards and there were many people in the street. I went running to see. A crowd was following a tall blond man who was leading a boy of ten by the hand. He was wearing light gray trousers and a dark blue jacket. He passed by me and gave me an embrace. I was bewildered by that embrace without even being introduced. It was the first time I'd ever seen the man.

Coca Cola's brother-in-law told me:

"That's our Congressman, Dr. Contrini."

When he said Congressman I thought: it's election time, that's why they're all so friendly.

Senhor Contrini came to tell us that he was a candidate in the next elections. We of the favela have not been protected by you, Senhor Contrini. We don't know you, and you don't know us.

August 6 I made coffee for João and José Carlos, who is ten years old today. I could only give him my congratulations, because I don't even know if we are even going to eat today.

August 7 I got out of bed at 4 a.m. I didn't sleep because I went to bed hungry. And he who lies down with hunger doesn't sleep.

I saw the tax collector wandering around and asking questions. I went to see what he was doing. He was looking for Senhor Tiburcio. He builds shacks to sell and begs over on Direita Street. He doesn't need to and doesn't live in the favela. He has already built seven shacks and sold them. Tiburcio has a deformed body and a soul to match.

When João got home from school I gave him lunch. Later we went to the city. We walked because I didn't have money

to pay for transportation. I took a sack with me and picked
up scrap iron I found in the streets. We went down
Cantareira Street. Vera stared at the cheeses and choked on
her saliva.

Dona Alice told me that Policarpo, a *nortista* that lives here
in the favela, brought a black woman to live in his house.
He told his wife that she was his cousin. His wife is very
good and she accepted the cousin in the house with pleasure.
And the cousin stayed there for several days. Policarpo's
wife would go out and he would stay at home with the
cousin. One day when Dona Maria returned to the shack she
found Policarpo and the cousin screwing. She didn't like it
and she fought with them. Policarpo left the house and went
with the cousin to Descalvado. He took the furniture leaving only the bed.

August 8 I left the house at 8 o'clock. I stopped at the
newsstand to read the major stories. The police still haven't
caught Promessinha. The bandit is foolish because at his age
he doesn't even know the rules of good living. Promessinha
lives in the favela at Vila Prudente. He proves what I've been
saying: the favelas do not form character. The favela is the
garbage dump and the authorities ignore that they have a
garbage dump.

I went to wash clothes. At the lagoon was Nalia, Fernanda,
and Iracema, who were arguing religion with a woman who
said that the true religion was that of the Believers.

Fernanda said that the Bible doesn't order anybody to get
married. That it only orders you to increase and multiply. I
told Fernanda that Policarpo is a Believer and has many
women. Then Fernanda said that Policarpo wasn't a Believer
—"he's just hot!"

I thought that was funny and I gave out a whoop. Something I don't discuss is religion.

I finished the clothes and left the discussion at its height.
Today the Welfare people were here twice, because Aparecida had an abortion.

Quita came to my shack complaining that José Carlos had
thrown shit in Marli's face and that I must give a better education to my son.

August 9 I got out of bed furious. With a desire to break
and destroy everything. Because I only have beans and salt.
And tomorrow is Sunday.

I went to the shoemaker to collect his wastepaper. One of

them asked me if my book was communistic. I replied that it was realistic. He cautioned me that it was not wise to write of reality.

Today the favela is spinning. Deputy Francisco Franca gave material to finish the clubhouse of the Blacks and Reds. He gave roof tiles and shirts and the people of the favela talk about this Deputy daily. They're going to give a party in his honor.

August 10 Father's Day. What a ridiculous day!

August 11 I was paying the shoemaker and talking with a black who was reading a newspaper. He was furious with a policeman who beat up a Negro and tied him to a tree. The policeman is white. There are certain whites who transform blacks into whipping posts. Is this policeman aware of the fact that slavery has been abolished or does he think we are still in the era of the whip?

I got frightened when I heard my children shouting. I recognized Vera's voice. I went to see what it was. It was little João, Deolinda's son, who had a whip in his hand and was throwing stones at the children. I ran and knocked the whip away from him. I smelled the stench of alcohol. I thought: he must be drunk because he never did this before. A boy of nine years. His stepfather drinks, his mother drinks, and his grandmother drinks. He is the one they send out to buy the booze for them. This time he had been drinking along the way.

When he got back his mother asked astonished:

"Is this all? What thieves those clerks are!"

August 12 I left my bed at 6:30 and went to get water. There was a long line. The worst thing about it is that malice is the main subject. There was a Negress there who acted as if she'd been vaccinated by a phonograph needle. She talked about her daughter and son-in-law who were constantly fighting. And Dona Clara had to listen to it because she was the only one who was paying attention.

Lately it has become very difficult to get water, because the amount of people in the favela has doubled. And there is only one spigot.

August 13 Everybody was telling that Zefa fought with a *nortista* woman. Swearwords came into action. I only feel sorry for the children who have to hear such language. Zefa is a mulatto and pretty. It's too bad she doesn't know how

All pictures by George Turok

Carolina inside her shack in the favela

Carolina with other favela dwellers

ABOVE: The child with her back to the camera is Carolina's daughter, Vera Eunice.

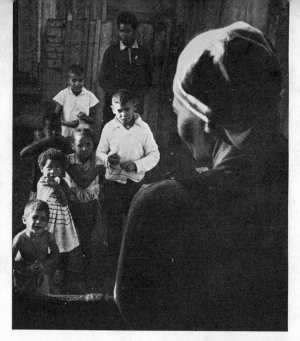

Carolina looking out the window of her favela shack

Life in the favela

Carolina looking at contractual papers with Audalio Dantas, the reporter who edited her diary for publication

Carolina waves good-bye to her fellow *favelados*. Next to her stand her son, José Carlos, and her daughter, Vera Eunice.

LEFT:
Carolina moves her possessions out of the shack as she prepares to leave the favela for good after the publication of her book. She is being helped by the Hungarian truck driver.

Carolina with a poster advertising the Brazilian edition of her book

Carolina walks to the river bank accompanied by Vera Eunice, João José, and José Carlos, on a return visit to the favela in November, 1960. They all are wearing new clothes, which are much admired by their old neighbors.

to read. She only drinks a lot. She had two children and she forgot to feed them. So they died.

I sent João to take a note to the Mello Brothers Circus asking if they would hire me as a singer. Then I went to wash clothes. I was getting ready to go to the circus when I heard rumors that Anselmo had shot Johnny Coque. I was writing, waiting for the rice to dry. I put away the notebook and started running around looking for Johnny. I found him seated on the Portuguese soccer field holding his legs with one hand and the bullet in the other. I asked him if someone had called the police. He said they had.

He was worried that there was no life in his leg. He tried to put on his shoes but couldn't. I gave him my slippers. The curious gathered. There were no comments. The people were only complaining about Anselmo. I'm going to tell you who Anselmo is. Afterward I'll tell who Johnny is.

Anselmo showed up here in 1950 with a woman who was pregnant. When the woman gave birth, to a boy, he started to mistreat her. He beat her and threw her out of the house. She cried so much that her milk dried up. Now he fought with Johnny because he is Iracema's lover. And Iracema's shack is near Anselmo's shack. And Johnny talks with his fiancée near Anselmo's house, which he doesn't like. He ordered Johnny to go make love near the river.

Johnny was at home drinking coffee when Anselmo called him out to talk. Johnny told him that he had just returned from work and he couldn't see him. It was then that Anselmo shot him. He didn't see Anselmo take out the gun. Anselmo aimed for the chest, but the bullet hit a leg.

Anselmo fled.

The people say they're going to get together and beat up Anselmo. Johnny went to be treated at Central Police Station and came back. I asked him if they gave him an anesthetic. He said they only gave him an injection against lockjaw.

It's just one more case for the police.

August 14   Ditinho, Lena's boy, is a veteran of the favela. But he's bald and never learned to read, never learned a trade. Only learned to drink *pinga*. Lena has a nicely built shack on Port Street. But Tiburcio tricked poor Lena. They traded shacks and he gave her a badly built one and kept hers. Afterward he sold it for 15,000 cruzeiros.

I went to the junk yard and got 15 cruzeiros. I passed by

the shoemaker to tell him to fix Vera's shoes. I kept hurrying up streets. I was nervous because I had very little money and tomorrow is a holiday. A woman who was returning from market told me to go and look for paper at Porto Seguro Street, the building on the corner, fourth floor, apartment 44.

I went up in the elevator, Vera and I. But I was so frightened that the minutes I stayed inside the elevator seemed to me like centuries. When I got to the fourth floor I breathed easier. I had the impression that I was coming out of a tomb. I rang the bell and the lady of the house and the maid appeared. She gave me a bag of paper. Her two sons took me to the elevator. The elevator, instead of going down, went up two more floors. But I was accompanied, I wasn't frightened. I kept thinking: people claim they aren't afraid of anything but at times they are frightened by something completely harmless.

On the sixth floor a man got into the elevator and looked at me with disgust. I'm used to these looks, they don't bother me.

He wanted to know what I was doing in the elevator. I explained to him that the mother of those two boys had given me some newspapers. And that was the reason for my presence in his elevator. I asked him if he was a doctor or a Congressman. He told me he was a Senator.

The man was well dressed. I was barefoot. Not in condition to ride in his elevator.

I asked a news vendor to help me put the sack on my back, and that the day that I was clean I would give him an embrace. He laughed and told me:

"Then I know I'm going to die without getting a hug from you, because you never are clean."

He helped me put the rest of the paper on my head. I went in a factory and later I went to see Senhor Rodolfo. I earned 20 more cruzeiros. Afterward I was tired. I headed toward home. I was so tired that I couldn't stand up. I had the impression that I was going to die. I thought: if I don't die, I'll never work like this again. I could barely breathe. I got 100 cruzeiros.

I went to lie down. The fleas didn't leave me in peace. I'm so tired of this life that I lead.

August 15 I was picking up manure to take to Ivani's house when I saw a truck on "A" Street, parked at Anselmo's door.

Florentina and Dona Lurdes came to tell Johnny Coque that Anselmo was going to move and for him to call the police. He couldn't walk because he was shot in the leg. So I went.

In five minutes the news spread that I had gone to telephone the police, to stop the moving of Anselmo. I returned before the police, and the *favelados*, as soon as they saw me, started to ask:

"Where are the police, Carolina?"

If I had saved all the money I've spent telephoning for the Patrol Car, I could buy a kilo of meat!

The people were waiting for Anselmo to make an appearance so they could beat him up. Men and women had collected for the beating.

I heard it said that Anselmo had jumped over the fence and got out the back way. I said that I would like to be a man, because I too would like to be able to break and beat. Then a man replied:

"I'd like to be a woman, but only during the day."

And everybody laughed.

Lalau and his mother-in-law had a fight. She hit him with the broom handle. She ran and he chased her. They were drunk.

August 16 I stopped by the shoemaker. Senhor Jacó was nervous. He said that if we had communism he would live better, because what his shop produced didn't pay his expenses.

In the old days it was the workers who wanted communism. Now it's the bosses. The cost of living makes the worker lose his sympathy for democracy.

The sack of paper was very heavy and a worker helped me to lift it. These days I've carried so much paper that my left shoulder is bruised.

When I was walking up Avenue Tiradentes, some workers came out of a factory and said to me:

"Carolina, you like to write, urge the people to adopt another regime."

A worker asked me:

"Is it true that you eat what you find in the garbage?"

"The cost of living forces us not to be squeamish of anything. We have to imitate the animals."

August 17 When I went to lunch I got nervous because I didn't have coffee. I started to get upset. I saw a newspaper that had a picture of Deputy Conceição da Costa Neves.

I tore it and put it in the fire. During the election campaigns she says she fights for us.

August 18   I don't like to lose a Monday. I go out early because I always find many things in the garbage. I left with Vera. I feel so sorry for my daughter!

I went to Dona Julita, picked up her paper. I earned 55 cruzeiros. What does 55 cruzeiros buy?

I was nervous. When I got home I lay down because I had carried some thirty kilos of scrap and tin cans. On my head. After I rested for a while I went to Rosalina to ask for her wagon to take the scrap to the junk yard. She loaned it to me and I filled the wagon. I was cold. I was welcomed with joy by Senhor Manuel. We weighed the material and I got 191 cruzeiros.

I went by the Guiné Bakery and bought a *guaraná*[22] and some bananas. I put Vera in the wagon. When I got to the favela I was beat. João said to me:

"Now that you've got some money, I can have my tooth pulled, because it's aching."

I told him to get dressed and wash his feet.

I was going to go out dirty. Then I thought: It's better to change. I changed, then hurried out. When I got to Filisberto de Carvalho Street I heard them talking about a fight. I went to see. It was Meiry, Pitita, Valdemar, and Armin. The Portuguese who sells cows' intestines had sold everything and was going home. He knows Meiry and he stopped to talk to her. Valdemar showed up and asked to borrow his bicycle to ride around on. The Portuguese replied:

"You want a bicycle, buy one."

And that began the exchange of insults. Valdemar, as he is used to doing to the *favelados,* gave the Portuguese a slap. The Portuguese socked Valdemar and threw him on the ground. Armin was on Valdemar's side and threw a brick at the Portuguese's head, who tumbled and his billfold fell from his pocket. When the *favelados* saw the billfold they went crazy. They all rushed at the same time to grab the billfold. When I got near Tiburcio's Ana, I asked her what happened, and she started to explain. And Isabel laughed and said:

"It seemed like it was raining money!"

[22] *Guaraná:* the Brazilian Coca-Cola, made from a tree in the Amazon jungle.

I ran near Valdemar and Armin who were smiling as if they had just done a noble deed. At a distance I saw the Portuguese who was covered with blood. And Valdemar said:

"It wasn't anything, Dona Carolina."

I said to Armin:

"Give the money back to the Portuguese."

He answered me:

"I don't know anything about it."

When I got near the Portuguese, Meiry was giving him the billfold. And the Portuguese said:

"The money is gone."

There was a white girl near Meiry, who called to her:

"Meiry, let's go."

The Portuguese gave a piece of meat to Meiry. It was a heart.

I took João to the dentist. I saw a sign on 2 Itaqui Street. Dentist. Dr. Paulo de Oliveira Porto.

I rang the bell and went in. A woman came to attend me. I sat down and waited. But I was worried about the children that I had left alone. Dr. Paulo came out and I told him that he is the dentist nearest to the favela and that I wanted him to remove a tooth from my son João. João sat down in the chair.

"How much is it, Doctor?"

"A hundred cruzeiros."

I thought the price was exorbitant. But he was already sitting in the chair.

I opened my purse and sat down, and started to count out bills of five. I separated 20 bills of five.

August 19 I didn't sleep. I got out of bed nervous. I went to get water.

The soldier Flausino told me that C was his father's woman. That she told him she went with his father and got 50 cruzeiros.

I commented on it at the spigot and the women said they had been suspicious all along.

Day by day the lives of the *favelados* worsen with the water line.

Vera is happy because I bought a pair of rope sandals for her. This morning she cried because her shoes had holes.

August 20 I went out to look for paper. I didn't talk to anybody. I met the city tax collector who joked with Vera saying that she was his girl friend. He gave her one cruzeiro and asked for a hug.

I got a splinter in my foot and stopped to take it out. Afterward I wrapped a rag around my foot. I found some tomatoes and went toward home. Today I am animated. Seems as if the old parts of my body have been changed for new ones. Only my soul is sad.

I came to the farthest part of Canindé. I went by COAP, a state-owned market, to buy some rice. The cheapest, which is already old and with the taste of dust.

August 21   I fixed coffee and made the children wash themselves for school. Afterward I went out to pick up paper. I passed the slaughterhouse and Vera went in to beg for a sausage. I only earned 55 cruzeiros. When I got back I sat thinking of my life. Brazil is predominated by the whites. But for many things they need the blacks and the blacks need them. While I was getting ready to make supper I heard Juana's voice asking me for a bit of garlic. I gave her five pieces. Then when I was fixing supper I didn't have any salt. She gave me a little.

August 22   I got out of bed at 5 o'clock and went to carry water. The line was already enormous. I only had four cruzeiros and an empty milk bottle. I went to Senhor Eduardo; he kept the bottle and the four cruzeiros and gave me a bread roll. I thought it was very little, but the money was also very little.

I made coffee and got the children ready to go to school. I went looking for paper. I found some rags to sell. I went by a house on Avenue Tiradentes and carried 50 kilos of paper that a woman asked me to sell for her. I put it on my head and sold it. It got 100 cruzeiros. She was pleased.

There are days when I envy the life of the birds. I'm so nervous that I'm afraid I'm going crazy.

August 23   Today there are no classes because it's the day when the teachers get together with the parents. I plan to go. I went out and took the three children. Today they are so refined. They're not fighting. Even I am calmer. I can see the transformation in myself.

I passed the slaughterhouse to get some bones. In the beginning they used to give us meat. Now they give us bones. I am always shocked with the patience of the poor woman who is happy with any old thing.

The children were content because they got a sausage. I

continued on to the junk yard. I found some cans, I spotted them in a field. When I was crossing the railroad tracks I looked to see if a train was coming and I saw Dona Armanda. I asked her if her son Aldo had left a notebook for me that he'd promised.

There was a lot of paper in the streets and I got 100 cruzeiros. I bought a sandwich for the kids. They like to go out with me because I buy things for them to eat. A mother is always worried that her children are hungry.

I washed the dishes and swept the shack. I wrote a little. I felt tired, so I slept. I woke many times during the night with the fleas that invade our houses, and without an invitation too!

August 24 I washed clothes. There was little soap. Dona Dolores gave me a few pieces. I started to feel dizzy, because I was hungry.

I went to see Chica. She told me that Policarpo had come to fight with his wife because she had complained about him to the relief board.

Corça told me that the Portuguese that Armin and Valdemar had attacked threw a sack in Valdemar's face and while he was trying to free himself from it, the Portuguese grabbed a board and gave him a few whacks, and they ran.

João and José Carlos went to the movie at Pari church. Today I'm not feeling well. I washed all the clothes, because I don't know if tomorrow I'm going to wake up sick or not. I don't know who is the miserable character who entered my shack to steal. Because my hatchet is gone.

August 25 I went to look for water and made coffee. I didn't buy bread. I didn't have money. I was going to take the children out when I saw a girl on her way to school and I asked her if there was going to be classes. She said yes. I dressed José Carlos and João went the way he was. I promised to bring them some lunch. I went out with Vera. There was no paper in the streets because another man had picked it all up. I did find some scrap metal.

August 26 I returned to the favela and cooked some food. I was ill. I lunched and laid down. I slept. What a luxurious sleep! Without dreams, without nightmares.

I woke up with the voice of the *Baiana* woman who was scolding my sons and throwing rocks at the other children. Here in the favela nobody likes her because she is always fighting with the children. I went to talk to Dona Alice. I am very unhappy. She told me that Pitita had been fighting with a man and called his mother a cheap whore. The man reported her and the police came to get her. She fled.

August 27 Dona Irene gave me some newspapers. I sold them and got 30 cruzeiros. I sold some newspapers belonging to a teacher and got 40 cruzeiros. She gave me half of it. I earned five more. All together I had 55, I went by the factory to pick up some tomatoes. I got back home and asked to borrow Rosalina's wagon to look for wood so I could make a pigpen. I took Vera and José Carlos with me. I just tramped around, mostly killing time. After I work and earn enough money for my children, I'm going to rest. A justifiable rest.

August 28 I went to get water. What a line! When I saw the line of cans I became depressed with life. I left my cans in line and went back to make some coffee. I woke João. He washed himself and went out to buy bread. I washed the dishes and disinfected José Carlos. I changed his clothes and gave him coffee. Then they went to school. I went back to the spigot. There were some arguments because some had tried to get ahead of the others.

August 30 I went by the slaughterhouse and they gave me some bones. At the junk yard I got ten cruzeiros. I circled back by Porto Seguro Street and I met that blond boy, tall and pretty. The type of man that women like to hug. He stopped to greet me.

I went to Senhor Eduardo to buy kerosene, oil, and ink to write with.

While I was waiting for the ink, a white man that was nearby asked me if I knew how to read. I told him I did. Then he picked up a pencil and wrote:

"Are you married? If not, would you like to sleep with me?" I read it and handed it back to him, without saying anything.

August 31 They say there's going to be a dance because of the baptism of Leila's girl. They are already singing and drinking.

September 1 I went to the market and bought an orange. I returned home and Vera was out of the yard. I gave her a beating.

September 2 I made a fire and warmed up some food for the children because I don't have any money to buy bread. I changed the boys and they went to school, and I took Vera out with me. I almost went crazy. Because there was so little paper in the streets. Now even the garbagemen steal what the paper pickers could take. Those egoists! In Paulino Guimarães Street there is a metal shop. Every day they put their trash in the street and the trash has a lot of metal. I used to pick out the scrap and sell it. Now the garbage truck, before starting its regular collection, comes down Paulino Guimarães Street, picks up the trash, and puts it inside the car. Selfish! They have a good job, hospital, drugstore, doctors. And they are allowed to sell anything they find in the garbage. They could leave the scrap for me.

I spent the afternoon flattening the cans. Then I went to Bela Vista to get a box. When I went by the slaughterhouse the bone truck was parked there. I asked the driver for some bones. He let me have one that I picked out. It had a lot of fat on it.

I made some soup and started to write. The night arrived. João ate and laid down. I put Vera in her crib. José Carlos was in the street, hiding from me, afraid of getting a beating. He is just like a pig. He covered his shirt with mud. I made a pigpen and I'm going to put him in to live with the pig. It would serve him right.

Pitoca went through the streets inviting the public to see a movie. She called João, and I told her he was sleeping. I went to see the movie. It was about the church.

At the playground that Adhemar put here for the children, at night the riff-raff play. Bobo made so much noise that he interrupted the film. The *favelados* stepped on the electric wire and stopped the projector. The *favelados* themselves say that the *favelado* is stupid. I thought: I'm going to write.

While I was returning home I met Paulo who lives with Dona Aurora. She has a light-skinned mulatto daughter. She says that Paulo is the father. But her features don't show it.

I slept and had a marvelous dream. I dreamt I was an angel. My dress was billowing and had long pink sleeves. I went from earth to heaven. I put stars in my hands and played with them. I talked to the stars. They put on a show in my honor. They danced around me and made a luminous path.

When I woke up I thought: I'm so poor. I can't afford to go to a play so God sends me these dreams for my aching soul. To the God who protects me, I send my thanks.

September 3 Yesterday we ate badly. Today worse.

September 8 Today I'm happy. I'm laughing without any reason. I'm singing. When I sing I make up the verses. I sing until I get tired of the song. Today I made this song:

> There is a voodoo curse on you
> And who did it, I know who.
> It was little Mary
> The one you loved before.
> She said she loved you too
> But you showed her the door.

September 9 There was no school today because the President of Italy is coming to São Paulo. I didn't go out because it's raining. I spent all day writing. In the afternoon I made a soup of rice and beans.

September 14 Today is the Easter of Moses. The God of the Jews. The same God who keeps the Jews free even today. The black is persecuted because his skin is the color of night. And the Jew because he's intelligent. Moses, when he saw the Jews barefoot and ragged, prayed asking God to give them comfort and wealth. And that is why almost all the Jews are rich.

Too bad we blacks don't have a prophet to pray for us.

September 18 Today I'm happy. I'm trying to learn how to live with a calm spirit because for these last few days I've had enough to eat.

When I saw the workers in the factory B . . . I looked at the company name they have sewn on their backs and wrote these verses:

> Some men in São Paulo
> Walk with lettering on their back
> On them is plainly written
> Where they're working at

September 19 At the slaughterhouse they don't put garbage in the streets any more because of the women who look for rotten meat and eat it.

September 20 I went to the store and took 44 cruzeiros with me. I bought a kilo of sugar, one of beans, and two eggs. I had two cruzeiros left over. A woman who was shopping spent 43 cruzeiros. And Senhor Eduardo said: "As far as spending money goes, you two are equal."

I said:

"She's white. She's allowed to spend more."

And she said:

"Color is not important."

Then we started to talk about prejudice. She told me that in the United States they don't want Negroes in the schools.

I kept thinking: North Americans are considered the most civilized. And they have not yet realized that discriminating against the blacks is like trying to discriminate against the sun. Man cannot fight against the products of Nature. God made all the races at the same time. If he had created Negroes after the whites, the whites should have done something about it then.

September 23 I went to see Dona Julita. She gave me food. She is worried because Senhor João is sick. He says he does not hate those who harm him, that he, being poor, has seen many nobles among the poor.

I know that among the rich there is always a dissension because of money questions. But I can't answer these questions because I'm poor as a rat.

September 25 I didn't sleep because I was exhausted. I even thought I was going to die. I had the impression I was in a desert. There are times when I hate that reporter Audalio Dantas.[23] If he hadn't taken my notebooks I would have sent them to the United States and everything would have been over by now.

I got up two times to kill the mosquitoes.

When I was talking to Chica, Policarpo's "companion" called me. I didn't go. She went back inside her house and returned with a summons and gave it to me. It was for me to go to the Investigation Board tomorrow, the 26th, and take João.

It was on July 8th, 1958 when she told me that my son João of eleven years had tried to rape her daughter. And she never pressed charges until today.

September 26 I got a meal ready for the boys They came home for lunch, I changed them and took them to the Board. The Board decided to rent an automobile to take us to 3 Asdrubal do Nascimento Street.

We were seven people in that car. I felt sorry for a young girl that was with us. She told me that her mother had been dead a year. That her father had started looking at her in a

---

[23] The Brazilian reporter who discovered Carolina.

way that shocked her. And that she is frightened to stay alone with him in the house.

We arrived at Asdrubal do Nascimento Street. I went to talk to a woman who wanted to know what had happened with João.

She asked João if he knew what it was to make "Dirty-Dirty." He said he knew.

And if he had made "Dirty-Dirty" with that girl. He said he hadn't.

The woman stopped writing and read some papers. Then she proceeded with the questioning. She used slang with the boy. And the questions were obscene, wanting the boy to describe in detail his sexual pleasures.

I thought the interrogation was horrible. Vera and José Carlos were near enough to hear what the woman said. When she spoke I had the impression I was back in the favela.

September 30 I am waiting for the Justice official, Senhor Feliciano Godoy. He gave me some summons to distribute here in the favela. I didn't go to Isabel's because those who drink don't obey. She had made peace with her Negro.

For her, today is a day of love.

October 3 I got out of bed at 5 o'clock because I want to vote. In the streets all you see are ballots on the ground. I thought of the wastefulness that elections cause in Brazil. I think it's more difficult to vote than to register. And there was a line. Vera started to cry saying she was hungry. The man presiding at the table told me that in the elections you couldn't bring children. I replied I didn't have anyone to leave her with.

October 4 I left the bed upset because I didn't sleep. A neighbor is an intense Adhemar fan and spent all night with the radio on.

I passed the slaughterhouse to pick up some bones. Thanks to the elections there was a lot of paper in the streets. The radios are transmitting the electoral results. The ballot boxes favor Senhor Carvalho Pinto.[24]

October 7 A child died here in the favela. He was two months old. If he had lived he would have gone hungry.

October 12 There was a fight here in the favela because the man who owns the electricity wants 30 cruzeiros an outlet.

[24] Carvalho Pinto: powerful politician and currently Governor of the State of São Paulo.

I have been in the world for such a long time that I am sickening of life. Besides, with the hunger that I experience, who could live happy?

October 16   You all know that I go to get water every morning. Now I'm going to change my diary a bit and just write of what happens to me during the day.

October 17   I did my chores and went out with Vera. I went to Dona Julita to get a bed that she had given me. She is happier because her husband is better. While I was talking with Dona Julita inside the house, two boys carried off the bed.

I ran, caught the boys, and took back the bed. I carried it to a Jew who buys used furniture. He examined the bed and said:

"I give 20."

"Not enough. The bed's worth more!"

"I give 25."

"Not enough. The bed's worth more!"

"I give 30."

"Not enough. The bed's worth more!"

"I give 35."

"Not enough. The bed's worth more!"

"I give 40. But it's not worth it."

I was starting to get nervous with our dialogue.

He gave me 40 and I started out but stopped in the doorway to watch Vera who wanted more money. She said:

"If you don't give my mother more money than that I'm going to take away the bed."

The Jew slapped Vera in the face and she started to cry. He told me:

"Give her a cruzeiro. I don't have any change."

After I had supper I felt ill and laid down. I dreamed.

In the dream I was happy.

October 22   Orlando came to collect for the water, 25 cruzeiros. He told me that nobody was permitted to be late with a payment. I gave supper to the boys and they went to lay down and I started to write. I can't write peaceably with the love scenes that are unfolding near my shack.

I thought they were going to break down the wall!

I was shocked because the woman who is with Lalau is married. I thought: what a dirty common woman. But man for man, her own husband is a million times better.

I believe that one man should be enough for a woman. A woman who marries must act normal.

~~This story of women changing men as if they were changing clothes is disgusting.~~ Today a free woman, with no obligations, can imitate a pack of cards, passing from hand to hand.

October 23 —Orlando lives doing odd jobs. Now that he has become the one in charge of light and water, he's stopped working. In the morning he sits at the spigot giving his opinions. I thought: he'll lose because the tongue of a woman in the favela is acid. It's not bone, but breaks bones.

Even Lacerda [25] loses to the favela women!

October 24 I made coffee and sent José Carlos to buy seven cruzeiros worth of bread. I gave him a note of five and an aluminum coin of two, this new money that is circulating in the country. I got worried when I started to think of money made of aluminum. Money should be worth more than what it buys. Goods should not be worth more than money.

> I dread and despise
> This money of aluminum
> This worthless money
> Put out by Juscelino.

I rested, made lentil soup with rice and meat. I sent João to buy half a kilo of sugar and the donkey bought rice.

He spends all day reading comic books and doesn't pay attention to anything. He lives thinking of the Invisible Man, Mandrake, and all the other trash.

October 25 The favela today is having a party. There is going to be a procession. The Fathers are sending an image of Our Lady. For those who want it, the image will stay 15 days in each shack. They are saying their rosaries in the park. The procession will go to the streetcar stop.

In Chica's shack they are dancing.

October 28 I. separated from her husband and is living with Zefa. Her husband found her with his cousin. Now I. has begun to commercialize her body, in her husband's presence. I thought: a woman who separates from her husband shouldn't prostitute herself. She should get a job. Prostitution is the moral defeat of a woman. It's like a building that fell. But there are women who don't want to be just for

[25] Carlos Lacerda: *see* footnote, p. 20.

one man. They want to be for all men. They want to be the only lady dancing the quadrille with many men. They leave the arms of one and go to the arms of another.

Dona Maria Preta brought her daughter for me to disinfect. Her mouth was covered with sores.

October 29   I got out of bed at 6. I was upset because I didn't sleep. I spent all night repairing the roof where it leaks. I fix one side and it drips in on the other. When it rains I almost go crazy because I can't go for paper or get any money.

I feel very cold. I put on three jackets and people who see me in the streets say:

"Oh, how fat you got!"

The era has passed when a person can put on weight.

José Baiano's woman told me, and begged me not to tell anything to anybody, that José threw her out of the house. They haven't spoken to each other for 20 days.

I told her to make peace, because José is a good man.

October 30   I went out with Vera. I noted an unusual amount of police in the streets. I talked with a city worker. He complained that he had to pay five cruzeiros on the bus.

I went on, looking at the *Paulistas* walking in the streets with sad faces. I didn't see anybody smile. You could call today The Day of Sadness.

I started to add up how much I would spend on the streetcar to take the children into the city. Three kids and I, 24 cruzeiros coming and going. I thought of rice at 30 cruzeiros a kilo.

A woman called me and gave me some paper. She said that because of the raise in transportation fares the police were in the streets in case of riots. I was unhappy. I could see that the news of the raise saddened everyone. She told me:

"They spend in the elections and afterward raise everything. Auro lost, up went the price of meat. Adhemar lost, up went bus fares. A little on everything, and they'll get back what they spent. It is the people who pay the election expenses!"

October 31   I went to get water. How wonderful! No line! Because it is raining. The women of the favela were upset and chattering. I asked what happened. They said that Orlando Lopes, now the owner of the electricity, had beat Zefa.

And she reported him and he was arrested. I asked Geraldina if it was true. She said it was.

Nena said that Orlando hit Zefa for real. I went for some paper. Vera went past the slaughterhouse and asked for a sausage. I earned 106 cruzeiros. Vera got six cruzeiros, because she went into a bar to ask for some water and they thought she was asking for money.

The people are saying that Dr. Adhemar raised the fares to punish the people because he lost at the ballot box.

When I got home the boys were already there. I heated the food. There was very little. And they stayed hungry.

In all the streetcars they've put a policeman. And the buses too. The people don't know how to fight back. They should go to the Ibirapuera Palace (the mayor's office) and the State Assembly and give a kick to these shamefaced politicians who don't know how to run the country.

I am unhappy because I didn't have anything to eat.

I don't know what we are going to do. If you work you go hungry, if you don't work you go hungry.

Many people are saying that we must kill Dr. Adhemar. That he is ruining the country. Bus fares are too expensive. It can't go on like this. Nobody can take it any more.

In the morning when I was leaving, Orlando and Joaquim Paraíba came back, returning from jail.

November 1 I found a sack of corn flour in the garbage and brought it home for the pig. I am so used to garbage cans that I don't know how to pass one without having to see what is inside.

Today I'm going out to look for paper but I know I'm not going to find anything. There is an old man who is in my territory.

Yesterday I read that fable about the frog and the cow. I feel that I am a frog. I want to swell up until I am the same size as the cow.

I see that the people are still thinking that we must revolt against the price of necessities and not just attack the transportation company. Dr. Adhemar told the newspapers that it was with an ache in his heart that he signed the raise agreement. Someone said:

"Adhemar is mistaken. He doesn't have a heart."

"If the cost of living keeps on rising until 1960, we're going to have a revolution!"

November 2 I went to wash clothes and stayed by the

river until 7:30. Dorça came to wash her clothes and we talked about the shameless riffraff that runs around the favela. We talked about Zefa who gets it every day. I mentioned the women who don't work but always have money. We talked about the love affair between Lalau and Dona M. But Dona M. says that he is having an affair with Nena. Nena is a jerk.

I washed the colored clothes and went to make coffee. I thought I had some coffee. I hadn't.

A thing that I hate to do is to go into the little room where I sleep, because it is so confining. For me to sweep the room I have to take the bed apart. I sweep the room once every 15 days.

Lunch was ready but the boys didn't come to eat it. João disappeared. I figured that he went to the movies. I ate a little and picked up a book to read. Afterward I felt chilly and went to sit in the sun. I thought the sun was too hot, so I went to sit in the shade. I talked with a man. He said there was a rumor going around that the favela was going to be torn down because they were going to put an avenue through here. He said it wouldn't be right away. That the mayor doesn't have any money.

João came home from the movies. I gave him a slap and he beat it fast.

November 3 I found some scrap. I left a little at the junk yard and the rest I took home. When I passed the newsstand I read this student slogan:

> Juscelino skins!
> Adhemar robs!
> Janio kills!
> Congress approves!
> The public pays!

I stopped near the train tracks to pick up some cans I had left near the watchman's shed and asked him to guard for me. The watchman asked me how much I would receive for the cans. I replied that it should be around 300 cruzeiros. I'm sick and tired of odd jobs. He said they were better than nothing. I told him that oil cans were 70 cruzeiros and now they are only 60. He said:

"Instead of going up, they went down."

He said that life is very expensive. Even women are more expensive. That when he wants to f— a woman they want so much money that he gives up the idea.

I pretended I didn't hear, because I don't speak pornography. I went away without thanking him.

I gave the children a bath and they went to lie down. I washed the dishes. Later I wrote. I felt tired and sleepy. I laid down. I killed some fleas that were walking around on the bed and laid down again. I didn't see any more.

I slept three hours straight. I woke up from the voice of Joaquim Paraíba, who was complaining that he had got a woman that didn't want to make love in the dark. She would only love him during the day, or at night near a light.

I thought: He doesn't have decent intentions toward this woman.

November 4 I went to pick up paper. When I was returning I stopped at a newsstand. I heard a man complaining that the police were donkeys. In a photo a policeman was beating an old man. I decided to take the streetcar and go home. We were talking about Dr. Adhemar, the only name that we can blame for the rise in the cost of transportation. A man told me that our politicians are clowns.

I think that Dr. Adhemar is angry, and he decided to be forceful with the people and show them that he had the strength to punish us.

But really superior people do not try for revenge.

I got home tired and with my body aching. I found Vera in the street. That blessed João, my model son, doesn't pay attention to anything. The shack was wide open and shoes thrown on the floor. He didn't put a fire under the beans. It was 6:30 when he showed up. I made him light the fire. Then I gave him a beating, with a stick and a belt. And I tore up those disgusting comic books. A type of reading material that I can't stand.

November 5 I went to the store and sold an empty bottle to Senhor Eduardo for three cruzeiros so I could pay on the bus. When I got to the bus stop I met Toninho. He works at the Saraiva Bookshop. I told him:

"That's it, Toninho, the publishers in Brazil don't print what I write because I'm poor and haven't got any money to pay them. That's why I'm going to send my novels to the United States." He gave me the addresses of some editors that I should contact.

Went on up the street picking up pieces of scrap iron I found.

At Dona Julita's house I asked for some food. She heated

some for me. Dona Julita gave me soup, coffee, and bread. I ate it there, in her house. It was 3 o'clock. I didn't feel good. The furniture was spinning around me. It's my body is not used to being invigorated.

I made soup for the children. They slept until it had cooked. When it was ready I woke them up to eat. We ate and slept. I dreamt about Dona Julita. That she had asked me to work for her and that she would pay me 4,000 cruzeiros a month. I told her that I would intern my sons. And only take Vera.

I woke up. I didn't sleep more.

I started to feel hungry. He who is hungry doesn't sleep.

When Jesus told the women of Jerusalem: "Don't cry for me. Cry for your own selves," his words were prophesizing the government of President Juscelino. A crown of thorns for the Brazilian people. A crown that the poor have to wear while eating what they find in the garbage or else sleep with hunger.

Have you ever seen a dog when he wanted to grab his tail with his mouth and kept spinning around without catching it? It's exactly like Juscelino's government!

November 6   When I got to Dona Julita's it was 8:30. She gave me some coffee. Vera said she would like to live in a house just like Dona Julita's. She made lunch. Vera ate and said:

"What delicious food!"

Dona Julita's meal left me dizzy.

After lunch was over she gave me soap, cheese, lard, and rice. That long-needle rice. The rice of people of property.

November 8   I went to the Japanese to shop. I bought a kilo and a half of beans, two of rice, and a half of sugar and one soap. I asked him to add it up. It was 100 cruzeiros. Sugar has gone up. The word in style today is "up." Up!

That reminds me of the four lines that Roque made and gave to me to include in my poetry book and say that it was mine:

> Politicians on their platform
> Promise they will give you raises
> And the people find out soon enough
> That it's their suffering that was raised.

I went to pick up an old wardrobe closet. A young girl

who lived there helped me to carry it down and she gave me
a mattress. I wasn't able to put the wardrobe on the wagon.
João was beginning to get nervous. He said:

"Damned hour when I came to get this wardrobe!"

The owner of a shoe store helped me put the wardrobe
on the wagon. It fell off because the wagon tipped over.
There were some men from the light company working. I went
up to one and he gave me a rope. I started to tie it. But I
couldn't do it. People stopped to look at me. João was nervous with their stares. I glared at the employees of the light
company and thought: in Brazil there aren't any more men!
If there were any they would fix this for me. I must have been
born in Hell!

I put the mattress inside the wardrobe. It was worse. The
light company workers watched my fight. And I thought:
That's all they are good for—staring. I thought: I didn't come
into the world to wait for help from anybody! I've managed
many things alone, and I have to manage this one here! I
had to do something about that wardrobe. I wasn't thinking
about men from the light company. I was sweating and I
smelt the odor of my sweat. I was startled when I heard a
voice in my ear:

"Wait a moment. Let me help you."

I thought: now it will be done. I looked at the man and
he was handsome. He took the mattress out of the wardrobe
and put it on the wagon. Then he put the wardrobe onto the
wagon just right so it wouldn't tip over. He took the rope and
tied it. João was boastful and said:

"Thanks to us men!"

I was cursing Senhor Manuel when he showed up. He gave
me a "good evening." I asked him:

"I was cursing you. Didn't you hear?"

"No, I didn't hear anything."

"I was telling my boys that I wanted to be black."

"Well, aren't you black?"

"I am. But I wanted to be one of those scandalous blacks
to beat you up and tear your clothes."

When he lets a few days pass without coming here, I start
cursing him. I say: When he arrives I'll hit him and throw
water on him. But when he comes I get weak.

He tells me that he wants to marry me. I look at him and
think: this man will not do for me. He seems like an actor,

just about to go on stage. I like men who can drive nails, who can do something around the house.

But when I am lying with him, I think that he will do. I made rice and put water on to boil so I could take a bath. I thought about the words Policarpo's woman said, that when she passed near me I was stinking like a codfish. I told her that I work hard and had just carried more than 100 kilos of paper. And it was a warm day. And the human body is worthless.

Anyone who works like I do, must stink!

November 9 I got lunch ready for the children and went to wash clothes. Dorça was at the river with a *nortista* woman who said that her daughter-in-law was in labor pains for the past three days, and she couldn't get in a hospital. They called the patrol car to take her but nothing had been done. The old woman said:

"São Paulo is worthless. If this was the North all I'd have to do would be call in a woman, and it'd be over."

"But you're not in the North. You've got to find a hospital for your son's wife."

Her son sells in the street market. But he doesn't want to spend anything on his wife because he wants to go back North and is saving his money.

November 12 I was going to go out, but I'm so discouraged. I washed the dishes, swept the shack, made the beds. I was horrified with so many bedbugs. When I went to get water I told Dona Angelina about a dream where I had bought a beautiful piece of land. But I didn't want to live there because it was on the coast and I was afraid the children would fall into the sea.

She told me that only in dreams can we buy land. In my dream I saw palm trees bending toward the sea. It was lovely! A dream is the most beautiful thing in the world.

Dona Angelina told the truth. The Brazilian people are only happy when they're sleeping.

November 14 I got out of bed at 5 o'clock and went to get water. There were only men at the spigot. Nobody spoke. I thought: if they were women . . .

November 15 The day dawned bright for everyone. Because today there is no smoke from the factories to leave the sky ashen.

November 17 I. and C. have started to prostitute themselves.

With 16-year-old boys. It's a lively game with more than 20 men after them.

There is a boy who lives on Port Street. He's yellow and skinny. Looks like a walking skeleton. His mother keeps him in bed all the time, because he is sick and gets tired easily. He only goes out with his mother to beg, because the sight of him touches people.

That yellow son is her livelihood.

But even he is following I. and C. around. So many young boys of 15 and 16 have shown up here in the favela that I'm going to report them to the authorities.

I saw the girls from the candy factory. So clean. I. and C. could work. They're not even 18 years old yet. They are unfortunates who started their lives in mud.

Today I'm sad. God should have given a happy soul to this poetess.

Pitita ran out with her husband right after her. The children watch these scenes with delight. Pitita was half naked. And the parts that a woman should cover up were visible. She ran, stopped, and picked up a rock. She threw it at Joaquim. He ducked and the rock hit a wall, right over Teresinha's head. I thought: she was just born again!

Francisca started saying that Joaquim was worthless. That he is only good for making babies. Leila shouted that Pitita was fighting with Joaquim because he was sleeping with I.

I. is being fought over in the favela. She left her husband. Leila in a fight is like gasoline on fire. She drags people into them like a spider with a web.

When Pitita fights everyone comes to see. It's a pornographic spectacle. The children were saying that Pitita had lifted up her dress. I went inside the house. I lie there listening to Pitita's voice.

The evening in a favela is bitter. All the children know what the men are doing . . . with the women.

They don't forget these things. I feel sorry for the children who live in the garbage dump, the filthiest place in the world.

November 20 I looked at the sky. It darkened as if we were going to have some rain. I got up, made coffee, and swept out the shack. I saw the women looking toward the river. I went to see what it was. I had some onions that Juana gave me because I gave her some tomatoes. I told

Vera to watch the onions and went to ask the women what there was in the river.

"There is a child that can't get out of the water."

I went to look. I thought: if it is a child, I'll cross the Tieté to take her out, even if I have to swim in the water.

I ran to see what it was. It was one of those wicker baskets they pack cheese in that was floating. I went back and started to write.

November 21 I saw many people in Leila's shack. I went to see what was going on. I asked Dona Camilia what happened.

"It's her daughter. She died."

"But what did she die of?"

"I don't know."

Tiredness overtook me. I laid down. I woke up with a crash near my window. It was Ida and Analia. The fight started back at Leila's place. They don't respect even the dead. Joaquim intervened asking them to respect the body. So they went to fight in the street.

This morning I told Senhor Joaquim Portuguese that the daughter of Dona Mariquinha didn't know how to read. He said:

"F—ing they learn. And without a teacher."

I let out a laugh and told him:

"Portuguese, you're hopeless!"

From my window I can see Leila's daughter in her coffin. The devils don't even respect the death watch. It looks more like a party.

The moon is marvelous. The night is warm. That's why the *favelado* is restless. Someone is playing the accordion, others are singing. A third of them are praying for Leila's daughter. The coffin is white. I'm going to lie down. The noise is great, but I'm going to lie down.

Here anything is a reason for an orgy.

November 22 I got out of bed at 5 o'clock and went to get water. I looked in Leila's shack. I saw José do Pinho in the midst of those tramps. I thought: such a beautiful boy . . .

Everybody is complaining that the wake for Leila's daughter was disgusting. That it went on all night and didn't let anybody sleep.

The hearse arrived to take away Leila's daughter. She started to cry. As soon as the child was gone, Leila began to drink.

I have to admire these souls in the favela. They drink because they're happy. And drink because they're sad.

Drink here is a comforter, in the sad as well as glad moments.

November 23 I got some scrap iron ready to sell at the junk yard. I made two trips. I earned 178 cruzeiros. I telephoned the Folhas to send some reporters to the favela to throw out some gypsies who are camping here. They throw their excrements in the street. People who live near the gypsies complain that they talk all night long, and don't let anybody sleep. They are violent and the *favelados* are afraid of them. But I've already shown them that with me the soup is thicker.

The girls run naked and the tramps sit near their shack, watching. The bad part is that if something displeases them, the gypsies riot. But their nudity is exciting. Right now I'm listening to a fight between gypsy and *favelado*.

I'll take our *favelado* vagabonds a thousand times to those gypsies.

November 26 I went for water. I looked at the place where the gypsies had camped. They only stayed three days, but it was long enough to annoy us. They are disgusting. The place where they were is filthy and has a foul odor. An unknown odor.

November 27 I am pleased with my literate children. They understand everything. José Carlos said that he is going to be a distinguished gentleman and that I'll have to treat him as Senhor José.

They have one ambition: they want to live in a house of bricks.

I went to sell paper. I got 55 cruzeiros. When I was coming back to the favela I met a woman who was complaining because she had been fired from her city job.

How horrible it is to hear the poor lament. The voice of the poor has no poetry.

In order to cheer her up I told her that I had read in the Bible that God said he was going to fix everything up in the world. She became happy and asked:

"When is this going to be, Dona Carolina? How wonderful! And just as I wanted to kill myself!"

I told her to be patient and wait for Jesus Christ to come to earth and judge the good and the bad.

"Ah! Then I *will* wait."

She smiled.

I said good-by to the woman, who was more cheerful. I stopped to fix the sack that was sliding off my head. I stared at a vacant lot. I saw the purple flowers. The color of the bitterness that is in the hearts of the starving Brazilians.

November 28 I went for water. There was nobody, just me and the daughter of T. (the woman who gets pregnant and nobody knows who the father of her children is). She says that her children are her own father's doings.

November 29 It was 11 o'clock when I went to bed. I heard loud voices. It was two women fighting. I heard the voice of Lalau. He's just gotten out of jail. He was locked up for three days because of Paulo's duck. I don't think that Lalau will ever again want his neighbor's ducks.

November 30 I saw a boy messing with his foot. I went to see what it was. It was a splinter. I removed a pin from my dress and took the splinter out of his foot. He went to show the splinter to his father.

The boy looked at me. But what a look! I thought: I've got one more friend.

December 5 Leila told me that Dona D.'s daughter has been arrested because her husband caught her in adultery with a *Baiano* that has two gold teeth.

Today I inaugurated a new radio. I played it until midnight. I heard the tango programs. Orlando turned on the electricity. Now I have to pay 75 cruzeiros a month, because he charges 25 per outlet.

December 6 I left the bed at 4 a.m. I turned on the radio to listen to the day dawn with a tango.

I was shocked when I heard the children saying that the son of Senhor Joaquim went to school drunk. The boy is 12 years old.

Today I am very sad.

December 8 In the morning the priest came to say Mass. Yesterday he came in the church car and told the *favelados* that they must have children. I thought: why is it that the poor have to have children—is it that the children of the poor have to be workers?

In my humble opinion who should have children are the rich, who could give brick houses to their children. And they could eat what they wanted.

When the church car comes to the favela, then all sorts of arguments start about religion. The women said that the priest told them that they should have children and when they needed bread they could go to the church and get some.

For Senhor Priest, the children of the poor are raised only on bread. They don't wear clothes or need shoes.

December 11 I was complaining to Dona Maria das Coelhas that what I earned wasn't enough to keep my children. That they didn't have clothes or shoes to wear. And I don't stop for a minute. I pick up everything that I can sell, and misery continues right by my side.

She told me that she is sick of life. I listened to her lament in silence. And told her:

"We are predestined to die of hunger."

December 13 A *nortista* woman was complaining that she and her sons are going back to the interior because they couldn't find jobs here in São Paulo. They're going to pick cotton. I felt sorry for her. I have picked cotton. I felt sorry for her.

December 14 This morning there was a Mass. The priest told us not to drink, for the man who drinks doesn't know what he's doing. That we must drink lemonade and water. Many people went to the Mass. He said that it was a pleasure for him to be with us.

But if that Father lived with us he would soon change his tune.

December 16 While I was talking with Senhor Venancio, I saw a disgusting sight. The wife of that mulatto who lives in front of Senhor A. was making love to João Nortista. That one that has two gold teeth.

December 18 I was writing. She asked me:

"Dona Carolina, am I in that book? Let me see!"

"No. Who's going to read this is Senhor Audalio Dantas, and he's going to publish it."

"Well, why am I in it?"

"You are here because of that day when Armin fought with you and started to slap you, and you ran naked into the street."

She didn't like that, and told me:

"What are you going to gain by this?"

I decided to go back into the house. I looked at the sky with its black clouds that were ready to turn into rain.

December 19 I awoke with a stomach ache and vomiting. Sick and with nothing to eat. I sent João to the junk yard to sell a few rags and some scrap iron.

He got 23 cruzeiros. It wasn't even enough to make soup. What torture it is to become sick in a favela! I thought: today is my last day above ground.

I felt that I had gotten better. I sat on the bed and began to look for fleas. The idea of death had faded. And I started to make plans for the future.

Today I didn't go out to pick up paper. Let happen whatever God wills.

December 20 The old people say that at the end of the world life is going to be empty and drab. I think that's pure talk, because Nature continues to give us everything.

We have the stars that shine. We have the sun that warms us. And the rains that fall from high to give us our daily bread.

I was getting ready to go to bed when Duca appeared, asking me to report Senhor Manuel, because he bought a television and the television captured all the electrical energy and left the favela without lights. She was wrong. The television wasn't even connected. Something that I never want to do is defame Senhor Manuel. He is the most distinguished man in the favela. He has been here for nine years. He leaves the house and goes right to work, never misses a day. Never fights with anyone. Never was arrested. He is the best-paid man in the favela. He works for the Count Francisco Matarazzo.[26]

December 24 Today I am lucky. There are many papers in the street. At 5 I got dressed to go to the Spirit of the Divine Master Center to get the Christmas handouts. I got the children dressed and left. I heard voices:

"They're giving out cards!"

I ran to see. I saw the *favelados* surrounding a car, and the people running. There was only the driver in the car. The people pleaded:

"Give me one. Give me one."

The driver said:

"You're dirtying the car!"

I asked him:

"What is it you're handing out?"

---

[26] Count Matarazzo: the richest man in São Paulo, if not all Brazil, who commands the biggest industrial empire in Latin America. His father arrived a penniless immigrant.

"I came to bring a man to the favela. I don't know what these people are asking for."

"It's Christmas season, and when an automobile comes here, they think you came to distribute presents."

"I'll never again come here at Xmas," said the driver looking at us with disgust.

There were so many people around the car that I couldn't even note down the number of the license plate.

At the Spirit Center the line was enormous when we got there. Ten children of a *nortista* were begging for bread. Dona Maria Preta gave 15 cruzeiros to her. She went to buy bread.

Senhor Pinheiro, the very respected President of the Spirit Center, came out to talk to the beggars. A man went by, stopped and stared at us. He said loud enough for me to hear:

"Is it possible that these people are of this world?"

I thought this was funny and replied:

"We are ugly and badly dressed, but definitely of this world."

I cast an eye over that crowd to see if they looked mortal or as if from another planet. The man went on smiling. And I keep on analyzing. When we got in to receive our gifts my number was 90. I and the others got presents and food: clothes, tea, potatoes, rice, and beans. Senhor Pinheiro invited me to come regularly to the Center.

It was 9:30 when we got to the streetcar stop and we went to see a crèche that they made in an empty garage. There was a sign outside that read: Free Entry. But inside there was a tray with a note of 1 and 100 on it. When I left I praised the crèche. The only thing I was able to do.

When I got back to the shack I found the door open. The moonlight was marvelous.

December 25 XMAS DAY. João came in saying he had a stomach ache. I knew what it was for he had eaten a rotten melon. Today they threw a truckload of melons near the river.

I don't know why it is that these senseless businessmen come to throw their rotted products here near the favela, for the children to see and eat.

In my opinion the merchants of São Paulo are playing with the people just like Caesar when he tortured the Christians. But the Caesars of today are worse than the Caesar of the past. The others were punished for their faith. And we, for our hunger!

In that era, those who didn't want to die had to stop loving Christ.

But we cannot stop loving eating.

December 26   That woman who lives on Paulino Guimarães Street, number 308, gave a doll to Vera. We were passing when she called Vera and told her to wait. Vera said to me:

"I think I'm going to get a doll."

I replied:

"And I think we are going to get bread."

I sensed her anxiety and curiosity to see what it was going to be. The woman came out of the house with the doll.

Vera said to me:

"Didn't I tell you! I was right!"

She ran to get the doll. She grabbed it and ran back to show me. She thanked the woman and told her that the other girls in the favela would be jealous. And that she would pray every day that the woman should be happy and that she was going to teach the doll how to pray. I'm going to take her to Mass so she can pray for the woman to go to Heaven and not to have any painful illnesses.

December 27   I tired of writing, and slept. I woke up with a voice calling Dona Maria. I remained quiet, because I am not Maria. The voice said:

"She said that she lives in number 9."

I got up, out of sorts, and went to answer. It was Senhor Dorio. A man that I got to know during the elections. I asked Senhor Dorio to come in. But I was ashamed. The chamber pot was full.

Senhor Dorio was shocked with the primitive way I live. He looked at everything surprisedly. But he must learn that a favela is the garbage dump of São Paulo, and that I am just a piece of garbage.

December 28   I lit a fire, put water on to boil, and started to wash the dishes and examine the walls. I found a dead rat. I'd been after him for days, and set a rat trap. But what killed him was a black cat. She belongs to Senhor Antonio Sapateiro.

The cat is a wise one. She doesn't have any deep loves and doesn't let anyone make a slave of her. And when she goes away she never comes back, proving that she has a mind of her own.

If I talk about a cat it is because I am happy that she has killed the rat that was ruining my books.

December 29 I went out with João and Vera and José Carlos. João took the radio to be fixed. When I was on Pedro Vicente Street, the watchman at the junk yard called me and said that I was to go and look for some bags of paper that were near the river.

I thanked him and went to find the sacks. They were bags of rice that had rotted in a warehouse and were thrown away. I was shocked seeing that wasted rice. I stared at the bugs that were there, and the cockroaches and rats that ran from one side to another.

I thought: Why is the white man so perverse? He has money, buys and stores rice away in the warehouse. He keeps playing with the people just like a cat with a rat.

December 30 When I went to wash the clothes I met some women who were discussing the courage of Maria, the "companion" of a *Baiano*.

They had separated and she went to live with another *Baiano*, that was their neighbor.

A woman's tongue is a candlewick. Always burning.

December 31 I spent the afternoon writing. My boys were bouncing a ball near the shacks. The neighbors started to complain. When their kids play I don't say anything. I don't fight with the children because I don't have glass in the windows and a ball can't hurt a board wall.

José Carlos and João were throwing a ball. The ball fell in Victor's yard, and Victor's wife punched a hole in it. The boys started to curse her. She grabbed a revolver and ran after them.

If the revolver had fired!

I'm not going to sleep. I want to listen to the São Silvestre race.[27] I went to the house of a gypsy who lives here. It bothers me to see his children sleeping on the ground. I told him to come to my shack at night and I would give him two beds. If he came during the day the women would transmit the news, because everything here in the favela is news.

When the night came, he came. He said he wants to settle here and put his children in school. That he is a widower

---

[27] São Silvestre race: a traditional footrace through the downtown streets of São Paulo every New Year's Eve.

and likes me very much. And asked me if I want to live with or marry him.

He hugged me and kissed me. I stared into his mouth adorned with gold and silver. We exchanged presents. I gave him some candy and clothes for his children and he gave me pepper and perfume. Our discussion was on art and music.

He told me that if I married him he would take me out of the favela. I told him that I'd never get use to riding in a caravan. He told me that a traveler's life was poetic.

He told me that the love of a gypsy is as deep as the ocean and as hot as the sun.

That was all I needed. When I get old I'm going to become a gypsy. Between this gypsy and me there exists a spiritual attraction. He did not want to leave my shack. And if I could have I would not have let him leave.

I invited him to come over any time and listen to the radio. He asked me if I was alone. I told him that my life was as confusing as a jigsaw puzzle. He likes to read so I gave him some books.

I went to see the appearance of the shack. It was pleasanter after he set up the beds. João came looking for me, saying that I was lingering too long.

The favela is excited. The *favelados* are celebrating because it is the end of a year of life.

Today a *nortista* woman went to the hospital to have a baby and the child was born dead. She is taking transfusions. Her mother is crying because she is the only daughter.

There is a dance in Victor's shack.

The DIARY of
CAROLINA MARIA DE JESUS
1959

January 1, 1959 I got out of bed at 4 a.m. and went to carry water, then went to wash clothes. I didn't make lunch. There is no rice. This afternoon I'm going to cook beans with macaroni. The boys didn't eat anything. I'm going to lie down because I'm sleepy. It was 9 o'clock. João woke me up to open the door. Today I'm sad.

January 4 In the old days I sang. Now I've stopped singing, because the happiness has given way to a sadness that ages the heart. Every day another poor creature shows up here in the favela. Ireno is a poor creature with anemia. He is looking for his wife. His wife doesn't want him. He told me that his mother-in-law provoked his wife against him. Now he is in his brother's house. He spent a few days in his sister's house, but came back. He said they were throwing hints at him because of the food.

Ireno says that he is unhappy with life. Because even with health life is bitter.

January 5 It's raining. I am almost crazy with the dripping on the beds, because the roof is covered with cardboard and the cardboard is rotten. The water is rising and invading the yards of the *favelados*.

January 6 I got out of bed at 4 a.m., turned on the radio, and went for water. What torture it is to walk in water in the morning. And I catch cold so easily! But life is like that. Men are leaving for work. They are carrying their shoes and socks in their hands. Mothers keep the children inside the house. They get restless because they want to go out and play in the water. People with a sense of humor say that the favela is a sailors' city. Others say it is the São Paulo Venice.

I was writing when the son of the gypsy came to tell me that his father was calling me. I went to see what he wanted.

He started to complain about the difficulties of living here in São Paulo. He went out to get a job and didn't find one.

He said he was going back to Rio, because there it is easier to live. I told him that here he could earn more money.

"In Rio I earn more," he insisted. "There I bless children and get a lot of money."

I knew that when the gypsy was talking to somebody he could go on for hours and hours, until the person offered money. There is no advantage in being friendly with a gypsy.

I started out and he asked me to stay. I went out and went to the store. I bought rice, coffee, and soap. Then I went to the Bom Jardim Butcher Shop to buy meat. When I got there the clerk looked at me with an unhappy eye.

"Do you have lard?"

"No."

"Meat?"

"No."

A Japanese came in and asked:

"Do you have lard?"

She waited until I had gone out to tell him:

"Yes, we have."

I returned to the favela furious. Then the money of a *favelado* is worthless? I thought: today I'm going to write and am going to complain about that no-good clerk at the Bom Jardim Butcher Shop.

Common!

January 7   Today I fixed rice and beans and fried eggs. What happiness. Reading this you are going to think Brazil doesn't have anything to eat. We have. It's just that the prices are so impossible that we can't buy it. We have dried fish in the shops that wait for years and years for purchasers. The flies make the fish filthy. Then the fish rots and the clerks throw it in the garbage, and throw acid on it so the poor won't pick it up and eat it. My children have never eaten dried fish. They beg me.

"Buy it, Mother!"

But buy it—how? At 180 cruzeiros a kilo? I hope, if God helps me, that before I die I'll be able to buy some dried fish for them.

January 8   I met a driver who had come to dump sawdust here in the favela. He asked me to get into the truck. The blond driver then asked me if here in the favela it was easy to get a woman. And if he could come to my shack. He told me that he was still in form. His helper said he was on a pension.

I said good-by to the driver and went back to the favela. I lit a fire, washed my hands, and started to prepare food for the children.

January 10   Senhor Manuel came over. It was 8 o'clock. He asked me if I still talked to the gypsy. I told him that I did. And that the gypsy had some land in Osasco and that if they tore down the favela and I didn't have any place to go, I could go to his property. That he admired my spirit and if he could, would like to live at my side.

Senhor Manuel became angry and said he wasn't coming back any more. That I could stay with the gypsy.

What I admire in the gypsy is his calmness and understanding. Things that Senhor Manuel doesn't possess. Senhor Manuel told me he wouldn't show up any more. We'll see.

January 11   I am not happy with my spiritual state. I don't like my restless mind. I keep thinking about the gypsy, but I'm going to dominate these feelings. I know that when he sees me he gets happy. Me too. I have the feeling that I am one shoe and just now have found the other.

I've heard many things said about gypsies. But he doesn't have any of the bad qualities that they blab about. It seems that this gypsy wants a place in my heart.

In the beginning I distrusted his friendship. But now if it increases for me, it will be a pleasure. If it diminishes, I'll suffer. If I could only fasten myself to him!

He has two boys. One of them is always with me. If I go to wash clothes, he comes along, and sits at my side. The boys of the favela get jealous when they see me pampering the boy. Pleasing the boy, I get closer to the father.

The name of the gypsy is Raimundo. He was born in the capital of Bahia. He looks like Castro Alves.[28] His eyebrows meet.

January 12   I made supper and gave it to the children. Rosalina came over. She came looking for a few beans. I gave them.

Senhor Raimundo arrived. He came for his boys. He watched the children eating. I offered him some supper but he didn't want it. He picked out a sardine and asked me if

[28] Castro Alves: Brazilian nineteenth-century abolitionist poet.

I had any pepper. I don't put pepper in the food because of the children.

I thought: if I was alone I would give him a hug. What feelings I have seeing him at my side. I thought: if someday I was exiled and this man came along to accompany me, it would make the punishment easier.

I asked Rosalina to eat the sardines. I gave her the beans. Raimundo told me that he was going away to his house, and that if one day the favela was destroyed, for me to look for him there. He gave the same invitation to Rosalina. I didn't appreciate it. It wasn't egoism. It was jealousy. He left and I kept thinking. He never parks. He has gypsy blood. I thought: if someday this man was mine I would chain him to my side. I want to introduce him to another world.

January 14 I walked through the streets. I went to Dona Julita. I went to the Blue Cross to get money for the cans. I got home before the rain. Senhor Raimundo sent his son to call me. I changed myself and went to him. He told me he was going to Volta Redonda to work in the steel mill. I know I'm going to miss him. I hurried away saying that I needed to write and it was something that couldn't wait.

January 15 I got out of bed at 4 o'clock and went to carry water. I turned on the radio to hear the tango program.

Senhor Manuel said he was never going to come back. He walked through the water to get to my shack. He caught a cold.

Today I'm happy. I earned some money. I got 300! Today I'm going to buy meat. Nowadays when a poor man eats meat he keeps smiling stupidly.

January 16 I went to the post office to take out the notebooks that returned from the United States. I came back to the favela as sad as if they had cut off one of my arms. *The Readers' Digest* returned my novels. The worst slap for those who write is the return of their works.

To dispel the sadness that was making me blue, I went to talk with the gypsy. I picked up the notebooks and the ink bottle and went there. I told him that I had received the originals back in the mail and now wanted to burn the notebooks.

He started to tell me of his adventures. He said he was going to Volta Redonda, and would stay in the house of a fourteen-year-old girl who was with him. If the girl went out to play he was right after her, watching her carefully. I

didn't like the way he was looking at the girl. I thought:
What does he want with this youngster?

My sons came into the shack. He was lying on the floor. I
asked him if he used a knife.

"No. I prefer a revolver, like this one."

He showed me a .32 revolver. I am not very friendly with
revolvers. He gave the gun to João to hold and said:

"You are a man. And a man must learn to handle these
things."

João told him he had better not say anything to anyone,
that he didn't want the people in the favela to know he had
a revolver.

"I showed it to your mother because she likes me. And
when a woman likes a man she never denounces him. I
bought this revolver when I was a soldier."

"You were a soldier?"

"In Bahia. But I left the corps because I was earning very
little."

He showed me a photo taken in uniform. When I got up
to go he said:

"It's early!"

He ordered coffee to be made. The girl said there wasn't
any sugar. I sent João to get some sugar and butter. He
sent his son to buy six cruzeiros worth of bread. He said:

"I never eat without meat. I never eat bread without butter. Here in this shack I eat. This shack made me put on
weight."

His boy returned with the bread. José Carlos came in and
started to fight with the boy. He told them not to fight because they were all brothers.

"I'm not his brother. Oh, no!"

"You are brothers because of Adam and Eve!"

He grabbed José Carlos by the arms, forcing him to lie
down beside him on the floor. José Carlos got loose and ran
into the street.

I put my eyes to the notebook and started to write. When
I raised my head his eyes were on the girl's face. I didn't
like the strange look he had.

My mind began to unmask the sordidness of this gypsy.
He used his beauty. He knows that women can be fooled
with pretty faces. He attracts girls telling them he will marry
them, then satisfies his desires and sends them away. Now I

understand his eying that girl. This is a warning to me. I would never let Vera in the same house with him.

I looked at the gypsy's face. A beautiful face. But I got nauseated. It was the face of an angel with the soul of the devil. I went back to my shack. I was putting the notebooks on top of the table when I felt someone grab me around the waist. It was the gypsy who was embracing me. He kissed me on the mouth. His arms were squeezing me tightly. He said to me:

"I'm going away. I'm leaving my clothes. You wash them for me. When I return I'll give you a sewing machine. I'm not worried about the cost. I know that if you think about me you'll miss me. I know that I have a spot in your heart. And you still will have the chance to sleep in my arms."

While he was hugging me, I was thinking: the place for this devil is in jail. I sat on the bed, he sat beside me. I shut the window and we continued kissing. My caresses were only there to discover his plans. He told me:

"I'm going to sleep here. The two of us will sleep, in this bed, and my sister will sleep in the little room."

"I don't sleep with anyone in front of my children."

He looked at me and said:

"You're stupid! Once children lie down, they go to sleep right away."

He went out. He was worried about the girl he claimed was his sister, not wanting to lose sight of her. He must be in the habit of seducing young girls.

He loves fooling around with them. He was interested in Dirce. But he didn't get Dirce because she did not see him up close. Because his beauty for women has the same attraction that bees have for honey.

He promised to come back. I want to introduce him to "Dona Justice." I called José Carlos. The gypsy was at the window. Pitita came near and said to him:

"You are very good looking, and I'll bet you'll like this!"

She lifted her dress. She was without panties!

The children stared and became quiet. The only one who smiled was the gypsy. I made supper and went to find Vera. She was in the store with the gypsy, who bought candy and sausage for his children and mine. I sent José Carlos to tell him not to come and sleep here. I was pleased.

Senhor Manuel arrived. He saw that I was nervous. He went away. I laid down, worried about José Carlos who was

still in the street. I slept until midnight. I awoke, thinking of
my boy who was still in the street. When José Carlos came
home I told him that I wasn't going to open the door and
that he could sleep in the street. He sat on the steps and
started to cry. It was 2 a.m. I opened the door, gave him a
bath, gave him some food, and he went to bed. I didn't go
back to sleep because I was super-nervous. I decided: when
the gypsy returns I'll present him to "Dona Justice." They
say that a gypsy cannot stop. But "Dona Justice" will make
him park a few days behind bars. I have had time to think
and re-think about what he said to me:

"You're stupid!"

He promised to bring me a present. And I promised to
give him one: a jail cell.

January 17   I got out of bed at 4 a.m., when I heard a neighbor's radio playing. I started to write. I turned on my radio
to hear the dawn come in with a tango. I awoke thinking of
the gypsy, who is worse than the Negro. I don't advise anybody to make friends with them.

I made a fire, washed the dishes, and went to get water.
I met Senhor Adelino and asked him about the gypsy.

"He fought with my brother-in-law. He said that he was a
Baiano and my brother-in-law said: 'If anyone here is a
Baiano, it's me!' "

I went to Dona Julita's. She gave me some food which I
warmed and ate. After I finished eating I became sad. It
was because the food was very rich. Soup, meat, and other
delicacies. When the poor eat rich food, they torture themselves.

Dona Julita knew I was sad because of the gypsy.

January 20   I spent the day in bed. I vomited up bile and
felt a little better. I went to get water. João was happy. He
asked me if I was better. I got pains and laid down again.

The boys are afraid that I am going to die. They don't let
me stay alone. When one goes out, the other comes to watch
over me. They said:

"I want to be near you, because when Death arrives I want
to give her a beating."

They are so well behaved. They whispered:

"If she dies we'll have to go to the Children's Shelter!"

José Carlos asked me if people can see Death arriving.
Vera begged me to sing for them.

José Carlos went to the street market to pick up things.

He found flour, tomatoes, and an eggplant. I ate some lunch and felt a little better. When I moaned the boys cried in fear of the Shelter. José Carlos said to me:

"You know, Mama, that when Death arrives I'm going to ask her to let us grow up and then she can come and take you."

To calm them I said that I wasn't going to die any more. They were happy and went out to play. Senhor Manuel arrived. He had come to see if I was better. I was pleased with his visit.

February 3 I have to tell you that I haven't written these past few days because I was ill. I'm going to recapitulate what happened to me during these days. Fernanda came to ask me if I knew where the gypsy was. It's the same as asking me if I know where the wind blows.

She said that he is very handsome and that she went there to buy pepper just to look at him.

During these days that I was ill, Senhor Manuel didn't let me go without money.

Senhor Manuel told me that the gypsy has great success in seducing girls of fourteen years. They trust him.

These days I wrote a few poems:

Don't you ever think you're going to get
My love again.
No, my hate will grow,
Put in roots and bear fruit.

February 15 Today I am much more animated. I'm laughing. We had a very funny brawl here in the favela. Leila started insulting the *Baiano* Senhor Valdemar. She ranted until 2 a.m. He decided to beat her. He went into her shack, broke down the door. When Leila tried to jump out, her foot got stuck on the window sill.

Today that Orlando Lopes came to collect for the lights. He wants to charge me, 25 cruzeiros for an iron. I told him that I don't iron clothes. He said to me that he knows I have an iron. And that he is going to connect a lead wire to the socket and if I plug in the iron it will blow the fuse and he won't turn the electricity on again. He said that when he turned on the electricity for me he didn't ask for a deposit.

"But a deposit has been against the law since 1948."

He said that he can charge a deposit because the light

company gave him special authority. And that he can charge whatever he wishes from the *favelados*.

February 16 When I was walking home I saw many people all looking in the same direction. I thought: a fight! I ran to see what it was. It was Arnaldo and a *Baiano*. Arnaldo was slapping him as if he were a child. I interfered and tried to separate them. Juana, the woman of Tiger Benny, came to help me. Many men were watching but not one of them tried to stop the fight. The *Baiano* gave two sharp blows to Arnaldo.

Then Armin showed up and said he was going to kill the *Baiano*. I tried to stop him, holding him by the arm. He gave me a push. I let him go, but screamed:

"Don't go, because the *Baiano* will kill you!"

I decided to call the police and ran away. I think I ran faster than Manoel Faria "The Racer." I arrived at the 12th District shouting:

"Fight in the favela! They are fighting with knives!"

I was disgusted with the idea of going back to the favela. But I had to return because I left my children there.

When I descended into Hell, the woman said:

"The police have gone in."

When I got back to the favela the crowd looked at me. Dona Sebastiana was criticizing. She was drunk. She said that she was going to cut off the *Baiano*'s head. I told her not to go in there because she would get killed. She started to insult me.

"You common nigger! You aren't a lawyer, nor a reporter, yet you have to mess into everything!"

The crowd shouted. The *Baiano* had gotten away.

Antonio, nicknamed Handsome, came out. He asked me if I had a pair of trousers I could lend him because his got wet when he went running after the *Baiano*. I started to look for a pair of pants for Handsome. I gave him the trousers and went out. I went to Arnaldo's shack to see if he had come back, because both he and Armin had been taken to the hospital.

February 23 In the street the people asked me what had happened in the favela. I explained I was unhappy because I didn't know the whereabouts of the *Baiano*. I wanted him to give himself up to the police. In the favela the gossip was flying. They were saying that Armin had died.

I was at the North Railroad Station. The *Baiano* showed up. He asked me about his wife, and I told him that she was staying with me, and that he could return to the favela because nobody had anything against him. He told me that he didn't have anything to buy food. I gave him 25 cruzeiros. He asked me if Armin was dead.

"No. He's in the suburb of Pirituba."

He said heavily:

"Ah! I'm no good. I didn't do a complete job. This business of hurting and not killing only serves to make an enemy. I don't know the man I knifed, and I don't want to go back there because he wants to kill me and the police want to arrest me."

"But you have to tell your side of the story to the police. If you had been arrested and I was near, I would have been a witness for you."

April 29 Today I am out of sorts. What saddens me is the suicide of Senhor Tomás. The poor man. He killed himself because he was tired of suffering from the cost of living.

When I find something in the garbage that I can eat, I eat it. I don't have the courage to kill myself. And I refuse to die of hunger!

I stopped writing the diary because I got discouraged. And I didn't have time.

May 1 I got out of bed at 4 a.m. I washed the dishes and went to get water. There was no line. I don't have a radio so I can't listen to the parade. Today is Labor Day.

May 2 Yesterday I bought sugar and bananas. My children ate a banana with sugar because I didn't have any lard to cook food. I thought of Senhor Tomás who committed suicide. But if all the poor in Brazil decided to kill themselves because they were hungry, nobody would be left alive.

May 3 Today is Sunday. I'm going to spend the day at home. I have nothing to eat. I'm nervous, upset and sad. There is a Portuguese here who wants to live with me. But I don't need a man. And I have begged him not to come around here bothering me.

Today the Father came to say Mass in the favela. He gave the favela the name of "The Rosary District." Many people came to the Mass. In his sermon the priest asked the people not to rob.

Senhor Manuel arrived and we started to talk. I told him about the girl of a year and a half who can't see anyone move his mouth without asking:

"What are you eating?"

She is the latest child of Tiger Benny. I can see that she is going to be intelligent.

May 4 I got out of bed at 6, because when Senhor Manuel sleeps here he doesn't let me get up early.

I was not born ambitious. I remembered this line from the Bible: "Do not horde up Treasures, because your heart will be set on them."

I've always heard it said that the rich man doesn't have peace of mind. But the poor doesn't have it either, because he has to fight to get money to eat with.

May 5 I wrote until 2 a.m. Later I went to carry water. I filled a barrel and the cans. I put water on to boil to skin the pig. I started thinking of what I was going to fix: smoked sausage, roast pork loin and pig skin with black beans. I was happy. I was going to eat meat. Really! I started to sing and sing.

I began to think, how long has it been since I've eaten pork? I went to see if Senhor Manuel was at home so he could kill the pig. He wasn't and I got worried. Senhor Manuel's brother, the owner of the pig, arrived. He had come to get his share. I had fed the pig hand in hand with him. I went to see Orlando Lopes and asked him if he would kill the pig for me. He said yes. I went home happy.

Orlando came over, went to the pen, and looked at the pig. As soon as the pig saw him, it gave a snort. It became nervous. I tried to secure him, but he was too excited. Orlando tied a rope to one of its legs, then dragged the pig out. Orlando gave him a stab. Seeing the blood run I grabbed a bucket to catch it to make blood sausage. I watch it gasping, not wanting yet to give up the last breath. Orlando stabbed it again. We waited for it to die. The minutes passed.

They skinned him and when they opened the pig I was pleased. The yard was filled with children. The women showed up, all saying they wanted a piece. Chiclé wanted the guts.

"I'm not going to sell, nor give. I fattened this pig for my children."

They protested. Maria, the mother of Analia, came over and asked me if she could buy some lard.

"I'm not going to sell any of it. When you fattened and slaughtered your pig, I didn't come around bothering you."

She said that all she wanted was some lard. I saw the looks in their eyes as they stared at the fat exactly like a fox when he stares at a chicken. I thought: and if they invade my yard? I decided to take the fat inside the house as fast as possible. I stared at the planks of the shack, which are rotten. If they force their way in, good-by shack.

I swear, I was frightened of the *favelados*.

Vera didn't go to play because she wanted to see us kill the pig.

The boys returned from school and asked:

"Mama, did you kill the pig?"

"I did."

"Ninho said it took three stabs and two clubbings."

The children smiled. I did too. I gave some pieces to Orlando and to Senhor Antonio Sapateiro. I made patties for the children. The meat was on the table. I covered it with a cloth. João said:

"Looks like somebody dead."

I said:

"I'm going to wash out the stomach, and don't you leave here, because of the cats."

Vera went with me. I went to wash it in the lagoon. José Carlos came along and I showed him how to turn the intestines inside out. Vera laughed watching the water run around inside the casings. José Carlos asked me if our bodies were the same as a pig's body. I told him that the insides of a pig were the same as the insides of a man.

"Then the pig was a man?"

"I don't know!" Stupid boy!

I returned home because I was tired. I knew that Maria was jealous because I had killed a pig. Vera wanted to eat supper, I cooked rice, and she ate it with meat. João ground up some pork and I put it on to fry.

João slept. I looked at his dirty feet that were hanging out of bed. I washed my arms and my greasy face. I brushed my teeth and laid down. It was 2 a.m.

May 6 At 9:30 the reporter appeared. I exclaimed:

"You said you would be here at 9:30 and not one minute late!"

He said that many people wanted to see him because they liked his articles. We got into a taxi. Vera was happy because she was in an automobile. We went to Arouche Square and the reporter started to photograph me. He took me to the São Paulo Academy of Letters. I sat in the doorway and put the sack of paper beside me. The janitor came out and told me to get away from the door. He grabbed my sack. A sack that for me has an incalculable value, because I earn my daily bread with it. The reporter said that it was he who had told me to sit in the doorway. The janitor said that he wasn't allowed to let just anybody who wanted to sit in front of the entrance.

We went to Seventh of April Street and the reporter bought a doll for Vera. I told the salesgirls that I had written a diary that was going to be published in *O Cruzeiro*.

May 7 I washed all the clothes. I swear I'll never kill another pig in the favela. I'm so nervous that I remind myself of my own proverb: "There is nothing worse in life than life itself."

Favela, branch of Hell, if not Hell itself.

For supper I prepared beans, rice, and meat. Vera is so happy because we have meat! When children of the favela see me they shout:

"Carolina, give me some meat!"

Dogs and cats walk around my shack. I am tired. I'm going to lie down. I awoke when Adalberto, who was drunk, came beating on my door.

"Carolina, give me a piece of that pig meat."

Oh how I hate this! And I am so sleepy! I listened to him sing. Afterward I went to sleep again. I awoke with something walking over the blankets. I turned on the light. It was a cat. I didn't go back to bed. I wrote until the first rays of the new day. Until I heard that man passing by shouting:

"Fresh bread! Get your fresh bread!"

May 8 I made rice and pork tenderloin, because I didn't have any beans. I took a bath, changed my clothes to go to the city. When I was leaving Vera came in and said that there was nobody working at the park playground school. The city runs it for poor children.

Before I went out I remembered that I had to give some food to the puppy. I looked at her, where she was lying. I gave a piece of meat and tried to wake her. She was dead.

Died from eating so much meat.

I went to the Welfare Board, to get the money that Vera's father gives me. I wanted to talk about it with one of the lawyers. The lawyer at the door didn't want to give me a number for the waiting line. The clerk told me: "Without a number I can't wait on you" and closed the door in my face. I told another lawyer that Dr. Walter didn't want to attend me without a number. He sent a guard to go with me and said:

"Very well, Carolina! Put all this in your diary."

I went with the guard, who told Dr. Walter Aymberé that he must wait on me without a number.

"I will not! If she doesn't have a number, I'll have to talk to the chief lawyer."

Vera got frightened and said:

"What a man! Why do people need lawyers, Mama?"

I told the guard to forget about it. I went away. Dr. Walter is now in my diary. He is very ill mannered.

I went to the Treasury to receive the money. When my turn came there wasn't any money. Vera wanted to buy a dress. I told her that her father had not sent any money. She was unhappy and sad:

"Mama, my father is worthless!"

May 10   I went to Dona Julita, and she gave me coffee and rice. When I was returning I met Dona Maria, that one who looks for paper at the gelatin factory. She told me that someone had stolen a sack of paper from her. I felt sorry. I met the Captain. I asked him why he left home. He answered me in a sad voice:

"You know, Carolina, I didn't want to leave my home. But the unthankfulness of my wife forced me to take the decision."

And he told me the reason. I said to him:

"She didn't make good business trading you for another."

He said:

"If I continued there, one day sooner or later, I would have had to kill that bastard."

I think that the man who broke up the Captain's home is worthless.

May 28   Life is just like a book. Only after you've read it do you know how it ends. It is when we are at the end of life do we know how our life ran. Mine, until now, has been black. As black as my skin. Black as the garbage dump where I live.

May 29   Adalberto got lost and went into the wrong shack. Instead of going into his he went into Aparecida's. And the *favelados* wanted to take him out of there, because if Negrão arrived he would have beat him. I went in to take him out, because he pays attention to me. He decided to leave. While I was putting him to bed he told me:

"You know, Carolina, life for me is now a bore. After Marina died, nobody loves me any more."

I laughed, because he had spoken and made a rhyme. But I stopped laughing, because the sadness in his voice touched me. Marina was a black woman who lived with him. She drank a lot. And died of tuberculosis when she was 21.

June 1 Today I didn't go to work because Vera and José Carlos are sick. I sold some scrap and rags. I only got 31 cruzeiros.

June 2 Today I'm not going out because the children are still sick. At 4 in the morning Vera started to cough. I got up and made some cornmeal mush for her.

June 3 This morning I only went for a pot of water. I made coffee and sent João to buy a bottle of ink and two needles. José Carlos is better and went to school. I left Vera alone. I have to go out because I have very few beans, salt, and just a half kilo of sugar.

June 4 Senhor Manuel came over. I'm treating him nicely now, because I realize that I like him. I spent many days without seeing him and I missed him. Absence sharpens the affections.

Dona Adelaide brought over my wool blouse and was surprised to see Senhor Manuel in the house. He is well behaved, he talks softly and dresses well. She looked at me, then looked at him. He with his gleaming shoes. And I filthy as a street bum. She was shocked that I sleep with him. She looked at me with disgust when I told her that he was going to give me a sewing machine and a radio. She asked him:

"Are you single?"

"I am."

"For the *senhora* he is very good, because he is single and the *senhora* is too."

I could see that her intention was to ridicule me in his eyes, calling me *senhora* (Mrs.). But she started too late, because our friendship is as strong as the roots that hold a tree to the earth. It is firm.

I slept with him. And the night was delicious.

June 5 When I got back home I made oatmeal soup. Vera cried. She didn't want to eat oatmeal. She said:

"I don't like it."

I gave her a slap and she ate it.

We laid down. At 10 p.m. the show started in the favela. Aparecida, the new neighbor, drank a lot and started to fight with Leila. Leila's boy friends wanted to destroy Aparecida's shack. She went to call the mounted police patrol. Adalberto came to Leila's rescue. He began to make a speech. When they heard the horses' hooves, they shut up.

Euclides, a black Negro who lives with Aparecida, is horrible when he drinks. He talks enough for a hundred people.

"I'll shoot them! I'll kill them all!"

When he stopped talking it was 3 a.m. A neighbor turned on a radio. I can't sleep with a brawl in the favela. Even the children were awake. I listened to the radio tell of a disaster on the Central Railroad.

In the morning José Carlos said he wanted to see a train wreck.

I told him:

"Don't think of that. The poor workmen!"

June 8 When I got home and opened the door I found a note. I recognized the reporter's writing. Dona Nena said he had been here. The note said that the article on me would come out on the 10th, in *O Cruzeiro*. That the book was going to be published. I filled up with emotion.

Senhor Manuel arrived. I told him that the article was going to come out on Wednesday and that the reporter took the book to be published.

"They earn money from your work and won't pay you. They're tricking you. You should never have given him the book."

I was not impressed with the skepticism of Senhor Manuel.

June 9 I told Mulata and Circe that the article would be out tomorrow.

"I'm going to spend 15 cruzeiros to buy *O Cruzeiro* and if I don't find the story, you'll have to repay me!"

I told Dona Celestina that Coca Cola's woman said that everything I write she writes too. Dona Celestina told me that she doesn't know if she can even write or not, but that she does know that I write.

I was reading stories to the children when there was a knock at the window. João said:

"Mama, there is a man here with glasses."

I went to see. It was Vera's father.

"Come in!"

"Where do you get in?"

"Go around front."

He came inside. He let his eyes wander around the shack. He asked:

"Aren't you cold here? Doesn't it rain in?"

"It rains, but I'm used to it."

"You wrote me that the girl was ill, I came to see her. Thank you for the letters. I thank you because you promised to protect me and not reveal my name in your diary."

He gave money to the children and they went to buy candy. We were alone. When the children returned Vera said she wanted to be a pianist. He smiled:

"Then you want to be somebody important?"

He laughed because his children are musicians. Vera asked him for a radio. He said he would give her one at Xmas. When he left I was nervous. Afterward I went out to buy bread for the children. They ate. And went to bed. I told Vera's father that I was going to be in *O Cruzeiro*.

He gave 100 cruzeiros. José Carlos thought that was very little, because he had other bills of 1,000.

June 10   Today I'm not going out because the shack is very dirty, and I'm going to clean it. I swept the floor and brushed down the spider webs. I combed my hair. The boys went to school. When they came back, they lunched. João went to take lunch to Vera. I told him to look and see if the article had come out in *O Cruzeiro*. I was afraid that the story hadn't been published and the people that I told to buy the magazine would say that I was making it up.

When João returned he said the story was out. I searched all my pockets for money. I had 13 cruzeiros. I lacked two. Senhor Luiz loaned them to me. And João went to get it. My heart was beating just like the springs in a watch. What would they write about me? When João came back with the magazine, I read it—"A Picture of the Favela in Carolina's Diary."

I read the article and smiled. I thought of the reporter and planned to thank him. I changed my clothes and went to the city to get Vera's money. In the city I told the news dealers that the story in *O Cruzeiro* was about me. I went for the money and told the treasurer that I was in *O Cruzeiro*.

I was in a hurry because I had left my children and the favela has a spirit of pigs. I took the bus and when I came to the last stop the newsman told me that the women of the favela were cursing me, that I was demoralizing the favela.

I went to the free park school to get Vera, and showed her the magazine.

I bought a half kilo of meat. When I returned to the favela I passed Senhor Eduardo's store. I showed the magazine to the workers at the slaughterhouse.

João told me that Orlando Lopes, in charge of the electricity, had been cursing me. He said that I owe him for four months. I want to talk to Orlando. He said that I put in the magazine that he doesn't work.

"What tale is this that I owe you for four months of light and water?"

"You do, you bitch. You tramp!"

"I wrote because I needed to show the politicians the worthless qualities you *favelados* are made of. And I'm going to tell this to the reporter."

"I'm not afraid of that pimp, that queer!"

What disgust I feel for that Orlando Lopes. I returned to my shack, made some meat patties and the children ate. I ate. Afterward I sang for them.

June 11 I got up and went for water. I changed the children, and they went to school. I didn't want to go out, but I have very little money. I needed to go out. While I was wandering through the streets people came up to me and told me they had seen me in *O Cruzeiro*.

I went to a newsstand and bought a copy of the magazine. I showed it to the druggist. I bought another and took it to show José at the Sport Bar. He bought the magazine. I went back and bought another. I showed it to the shoemaker. He smiled. I went by the store of José Martins and asked him if he wanted to read the magazine.

"Leave it here. Afterward we'll read it."

I fed the children and sat on the bed to write. There was a knock at the door. I sent João to see who it was and shouted:

"Enter, black woman!"

"She isn't a black woman, Mama. It's a white woman and she has a copy of *O Cruzeiro* in her hands."

She came in. A very pretty blonde. She said that she had read the article in *O Cruzeiro* and wanted to take me to the *Díario da Noite* newspaper office to get help for me.

At the newspaper I got choked with emotion. The boss Senhor Antonio was on the third floor. He gave me a magazine to read. Afterward he went to get lunch for me, steak,

potatoes, and a salad. I was eating what I had dreamed about!
I was in a pretty room.

Reality was much prettier than a dream.

Afterward we went into the offices and they photographed
me. They promised me that I would appear in the *Diario da
Noite* tomorrow. I am so happy! It feels as if my dirty life
is now being washed.

June 13 I went out and as I picked up paper, I heard
various people say:

"That's the one who is in *O Cruzeiro*."

"But how filthy she is!"

I talked with the workers. I broke up some cardboard
boxes and put others in the bag. I got 100 cruzeiros. The
women at the junk yard started to chant:

> "She came out in *O Cruzeiro*,
> She'll now get more cruzeiros."

Leon said:

"Did they pay you?"

"They're going to give me a house."

"Don't hold your breath waiting."

I met a black who is a neighbor of mine, Senhor Euclides.
He said to me:

"Dona Carolina, I like you very much. Do you want to
write many more books?"

"Oh, do I want to!"

"But you don't have anyone who supports you. You need
to work."

"I need to work, but I write in my spare time."

"I can see that your life is one long sacrifice."

"I'm used to it by now."

"If you want to stay with me, I'll beg for money and keep
you. Women like money, and I'll get money for you. I don't
have anybody who likes me. I am a cripple. I like you very
much. You are inside my head now and also inside my
heart."

When he tried to hug me, I pulled away.

June 16 Today there is nothing to eat. I wanted to invite
the children for a mutual suicide, but I resisted. I looked at
my children and was pained. They are full of life. Who
lives needs to eat. I got nervous and thought: has God for-
gotten me? Has he became angry with me?

June 18 Aparecida's shack is the meeting point for the drinkers. They drink and afterward fight. Lalau said that I put many people into the story, but I didn't put him.

"If you put me in the newspaper, I break you in pieces, tramp! This nigger must get out of the favela."

Aparecida came to tell me that my boy João told her to shove it up her ass.

I said:

"You people are the professors. When you drink you all say terrible things."

June 19 Senhor Manuel came over. He said he bought a copy of the magazine just to see my picture. He wanted to know if the reporter gave me something.

"No, but he's going to."

"I don't believe it. I'll only believe it when I see it."

I told him that only after the book is in circulation does the writer receive anything.

June 22 I left sad because I didn't have anything in the house to eat. I looked at the sky. Thank God it's not going to rain. Today is Monday. There is a lot of paper in the streets. At the streetcar stop I separated from Vera. She said:

"Make some food, because I'm going to come home hungry."

The sentence kept repeating in my brain:

"Food! Food! Food!"

They say that Brazil used to be good. But I am not living when it was good. Today I looked in a mirror. I was horrified. My face is almost like my departed mother. A tooth is missing. Skinny. Rotten! The fear of dying of hunger!

June 25 I went back to my filthy shack. I looked at the aging hovel. The black and rotten slats. I thought: it's just like my life.

When I was getting ready to write, that Orlando came over and said he wanted the money. I gave him 100 cruzeiros.

"I want 250. I want a deposit."

"I'm not paying a deposit because it was abolished by the light company."

"Then I'll cut off the current."

And he cut it.

June 27 That Orlando Lopes rode by here on a bicycle. My boys said:

"Look at Orlando!"

I told them:

"I'm not going to look at that repulsive creature."

He heard me and replied:

"The repulsive one is the whore that shit you out!"

I said that I had to write and couldn't waste my time on tramps. And closed the door.

June 29   Today I woke up hoarse. It was 4 a.m. when I went to get water, because that Orlando Lopes said he wouldn't let me get water any more. I put water on to make coffee. I only have 18 cruzeiros! I am so unhappy! If I could only move out of this favela! This place is the work of the Devil.

Wicked men have lived here, but that Orlando tops them all. I counted the number of shacks in the favela to see how much that Orlando will collect if the *favelados* pay him the 150 cruzeiros deposit. I counted 119 shacks with lights.

The sky is marvelous. Light blue with fleeting white clouds. The balloons with their many colors glide through space. The children get excited when a balloon floats away. How beautiful St. Peter's Day is. Why is it that the saints of June are honored with fire? [29]

That Orlando Lopes went down my street. He said that everything I say about him, the women tell him. They're a bunch of idiots. I want to defend them because there are thieves of all kinds. But they don't understand.

June 30   That black who picks up vegetables in the market came to sell me some withered sprouting potatoes. Looking at them I could see that nobody was going to buy any. I thought: this poor wretch must be wandering around hopelessly trying to get money for a meal. I asked him if he wanted some food.

"I do!"

He looked at me so tenderly as if he were looking at a saint. I heated up some macaroni, pig's lungs and cracklings for him.

July 1   I am sick and tired of the favela. I told Senhor Manuel that I was going through hard times. The father of Vera is rich, he could help me a little. He asked me not to reveal his name in the diary, and I won't. He can count on

[29] In the month of June, Brazilians celebrate the days of St. Peter, St. John, and St. Anthony with bonfires and skyrockets.

my silence. And if I was one of these scandalous blacks, and went there to his office and made a scene?

"Give me some money for your child!"

July 2 I got up, lit a fire, and sent João to buy ten cruzeiros worth of sugar. There was a knock at the shack. The boys shouted:

"It's the father of Vera."

"It's Papa," and she smiled for him.

I was the one that was not pleased with this visitor. He told me that he didn't take the money to the Welfare Board because he didn't have time. I showed him Vera's shoes that had holes where water came in.

"How much will you have to pay for this?"

"240."

"That's expensive."

He gave me 120 cruzeiros and 20 for each child. He sent them away to buy candy so we would be alone together. There are times when I am disgusted to be a woman. I thanked God when he went away.

July 3 There is no lard. Today I used the last of the pig lard. Now I have to buy it.

I took a bath and went to lie down. What a terrible night! That Terezinha and her "companion" didn't let us sleep. I don't know where they got a chicken. They argued:

"Go, Euclides, pluck the chicken!"

"You go!"

And they kept this rigmarole up until 2 in the morning.

July 6 Senhor Manuel left. I stayed in bed. Afterward I got up and went for water. What a chore! I listened to the women talking. They talked of D. who loves anyone. That R., sister of B., belongs to any man.

We talked of J.P. who wanted to make love with his daughter. He showed it to her and invited her to . . .

"Come, my daughter! Give some to your little daddy! Give . . . Give just a little."

I am tired of hearing about this, because unfortunately J.P. is a neighbor of mine. He is a man who cannot be allowed inside a house where there are children.

I said:

"And that's why I say that the favela is the pigsty of São Paulo."

I filled my can and fled, thanking God that I had left the

spigot. A.C. said that she asked her father to buy a pair of shoes, and he said:

"If you give me a . . . I'll give you 100 cruzeiros."

She gave. He gave her only 50. She tore the money up and I. picked up the pieces and pasted them together.

That's why I say that the favela is the Devil's Ministry.

I made lunch, afterward I wrote. I'm nervous. The world is so bitter that I want to die. I sat in the sun to warm up. With the harshness of life, we are the unhappy wanderers in this world, feeling the cold inside as well as out.

I felt myself perking up a bit. By the time night fell I was happy. I sang. João and José Carlos took part. The drunken neighbors interfered with their out of tune voices.

We sang the *"Jardineira."*

July 7 Dona Angelina Preta was saying that she is going to sell her shack and move to Guaianazes. That she can't stand living on "A" Street any more. I was pleased hearing her say she was going to move.

And I, the day I move, I'm going to burn incense to thank God. I'll make a mental fast and think only in good things that will please God.

July 11 It was 7 at night. The boys were in the street. João dashed in as if he was being chased by a Russian rocket. He said:

"Mama, José Carlos is going to the Children's Shelter!"

"Why?"

"He threw a rock through the window of the automobile parts factory and broke it. And the *nortista* who takes care of the place says he is going to send him to the SHELTER."

I thought: a window is a thing any other mother can pay for. I got up, put on my coat, took some money and put it in my pocket. I took the magazine with my article and went out. I went to see the window. It was broken, the rock had been fired with a slingshot. The hole in the window was oval.

The factory guard opened the window, saw João, and asked:

"What are you doing here?"

"It's me, and I came to see the hole in the glass."

The *nortista* started to talk. I asked José Carlos what he was doing there, walking around like a tramp looking for trouble. I asked the *nortista* if he had slapped him. He told me no. José Carlos said that he had squeezed his arm.

I believe in my son. In general, all mothers believe their children.

July 12   My battle of the day was to fix lunch. I didn't have any lard. I let the meat cook and put sausage with it to fry and clean the grease so I could make rice and beans. I seasoned a salad with meat broth. When Vera eats meat she gets happy and sings.

July 13   I bought 30 cruzeiros worth of meat and was upset because the 30 that was left over isn't going to buy lard and rice. I was afraid that my sons would fight with the neighbors.

When I got back they were sitting inside the pigpen reading comic books.

I heard Dona Adelaide's voice. She was saying to my son: "Have you stopped fighting?"

I asked Vera what had happened and who they had fought with. She said that João and José Carlos had been fighting with each other. That they let the guitar fall on the floor and put perfume on the fire to watch it flame. That they broke the floor scrub brush and opened a packet of green ink that I was saving. I don't know why, but I was saving it.

I put hot coals in the iron and ironed my green skirt, washed a knit blouse that I found in the garbage, took a bath and changed clothes. I changed Vera and we went to the city. I only had six cruzeiros. I thought: if the father of Vera did not deposit the money, how am I going to return?

I went to get Vera's money. What a line! They were women who had come to receive the monthly allotments from their husbands and the fathers of our children. I have to say "our children," because I was also in their midst. He who hangs on the vine also turns into a bean.

The women talked about their husbands. There, the men took names of animals.

"Mine is a mean, common horse!"

"And mine is an ass. That bum! The other day he took a trip on the Central Railway and I prayed to God to make a disaster so he would die and go to Hell."

I asked the woman who was behind me:

"Who is your lawyer?"

"Dr. Walter Aymberé."

"He's mine too, but I don't like him."

I got the great money. 250 cruzeiros. Vera smiled and said:

"Now I like my father."

We went to a shoe shop and I bought a pair of shoes for Vera. When Senhor Manoel, a *nortista,* tried the shoes on her, she said:

"Shoes, please don't wear out! Because later Mama has to work hard to buy another pair, and I don't like to walk barefoot."

I went by Senhor Eduardo's store and bought a kilo of rice. There was only seven cruzeiros left. In the city alone I spent 25. The city is a bat that sucks our blood.

July 15 When I got out of bed, Vera was already awake and she asked me:

"Mama, isn't today my birthday?"

"It is. My congratulations. I wish you happiness."

"Are you going to make a cake for me?"

"I don't know. If I can get some money . . ."

I lit the fire and went to carry water. The women were complaining that the water was running out slow.

The garbagemen have gone by. I got little paper. I went by the factory to pick up some rags. I began to feel dizzy. I made up my mind to go to Dona Angelina's house to ask for a little coffee. Dona Angelina gave me some. When I went out I told her I was feeling better.

"It's hunger. You need to eat."

"But what I earn isn't enough."

I have lost eight kilos. I have no meat on my bones, and the little I did have has gone. I picked up the papers and went out. When I went past a shop window I saw my reflection. I looked the other way because I thought I was seeing a ghost.

I fried fish and made some corn mush for the children to eat with the fish. When Vera showed up and saw the mush inside the pot she asked:

"Is that a cake? Today is my birthday!"

"No it isn't cake. It's mush."

"I don't like mush!"

I got some milk. I gave her milk and mush. She ate it, sobbing.

Who am I to make a cake?

July 18 When I was going out to pick up paper I met Dona Binidita, the mother of black Nena. I say black Nena because we have a white Nena in the favela. We started to discuss the boy who died on the wires of the light company. She told me he was the son of Laura and Vicentão.

"Oh!" I exclaimed. Because I knew the boy and his story of an unhappy life. Here is the history of the unfortunate Miguel Colona:

When Laura went to the hospital to have a child, hers was born and died. She was sad because she wanted to raise the boy. And she cried. Beside her a young woman had had a son. And she cried in envy of Laura. Because she wished that her son had been born and then died. But her son was alive. Those tears worried Laura, who asked her:

"Why are you crying? Your child is alive and beautiful."

The woman said that she had come from the North. A virgin. Here in São Paulo she got pregnant. And the child's father did not want to marry her. And now her parents want her to return to the North. She wants to go back up North, but she doesn't want to take the boy. If Laura wants the boy she would give him.

Laura accepted. She became as happy as if she had gotten all the gold that existed in the world. When she left the hospital she told people that her son had died but she had won another. She was good to him. She bought a television because he wanted one. He was nine years old and in the second grade. And now he's been tragically snatched by death.

We have only one way to be born and many ways to die.

Today there is a lot of paper in the garbage. But there are a lot of pickers in the streets. There are those that pick and lie down drunk. I talked with one paper picker.

"Why don't you save the money you earn?"

He looked at me with such a pitiful expression:

"You make me laugh. The time is past when people could save money. I am one of the unhappy ones. With the life I lead I can't have any hopes. I can't have a home, because a home begins with two but afterward starts multiplying."

He looked at me and said:

"Why are we talking of this? Our world is the outer edge of civilization. Do you know where I sleep? Under bridges. I'm going crazy. I want to die!"

"How old are you?"

"Twenty-four. And I'm sick of life."

I went on thinking: he who writes likes pretty things. Why do I only meet sadness and tears?

July 22   I was lying down. It was 5 a.m. when Teresinha and Euclides started to talk.

"Adalberto! Get up and go buy a bottle of *pinga*."

Euclides knew I was awake so he shouted:

"You're not going to write? You're not going to look for paper? Get up, so you can write about other people's lives."

I got up, grabbed a broom handle, and went to tell him not to bother me and that I am tired of working so hard. I gave the sides of the shack a few whacks. He shut up and didn't say any more.

July 26   It was 7 in the evening when Senhor Alexandre started to fight with his wife. He said that she had let his watch fall on the floor and break. His voice went higher and he started to beat her. She shouted for help. I was not moved, because I'm used to the shows that they put on. Dona Rosa ran for help. In one minute the news flew around that a man was killing a woman. He hit her in the head with the iron. The blood poured. I became nervous. My heart seemed like the pistons of a moving train. It gave me a headache.

The men gathered around to stop him from beating the poor woman. They opened the front door and the women and children invaded the shack. Alexandre came out of there furious and said:

"Get out of here, you trash! Do you think that this is a public restroom?"

Everybody ran. There were 20 trying to get out of the door. The children, he kicked. Vera got a kick and fell flat. The children of Juana were all kicked. The *favelados* started to laugh.

The scene was nothing to be laughed at. It wasn't comedy. It was drama.

July 28   I went to write. Nobody bothered me today. As dusk came on I went to get Vera. The *favelados* were gathered in the street enjoying a fight of Leila and Pitita with a little Negress who showed up here. But I am bored with fights. So many battles in this favela!

The light of Leila's shack was lit and the door was closed. There were many children looking in the cracks of the wall. I wanted to see. But there are certain things that an adult shouldn't do. When José Carlos came home he said:

"I've got something to tell you."

"What is it?"

"I saw Chico making monkey business with P."

I didn't show any interest in the subject. He persisted:

"Chico was making monkey business with P. and Vanilda was nearby watching everything."

Vanilda is two years old!

July 30 I wrote very late, because I'm not sleepy. When I laid down I went to sleep right away and dreamed I was in another house. And I had everything. Sacks of beans. I stared at the sacks and smiled. I said to João:

"Now we can give misery a kick!"

And I shouted:

"Go away, misery!"

Vera woke up and asked:

"Who is it you are sending away?"

July 31 I bought 20 cruzeiros of fat meat, because I don't have any lard. I went to Senhor Eduardo's store to buy one kilo of rice. I left the sacks on the sidewalk. Vera put the meat on top of the sack and a dog came along and took it. I cursed Vera.

"Worthless child! Today you're going to eat shit!"

She said:

"Stop it, Mama. When I find that dog I'll hit him."

When I got home I was starving. A cat came around meowing. I looked at him and thought: I never ate cat, but if he were in a pan, covered with onions and tomatoes, I swear I'd eat him. Hunger is the worst thing in the world.

I told the children that today we were not going to eat. They were unhappy.

August 1 I laid down, but I didn't sleep. I was so tired. I heard a noise inside the shack. I got up to see what it was. It was a cat. I laughed because I didn't have a thing he could eat. Then I felt sorry for the cat.

August 4 It dawned raining. I made coffee and sent João to buy 15 cruzeiros of bread. I borrowed the 15 from Adalberto. I didn't go for water. I'm sick of standing in that disgusting line.

I let Vera sleep. It was raining a cold mist. I found a pair of shoes in the garbage and I'm wearing them. When I went out for paper Dona Esmeralda asked to borrow 20 cruzeiros. I gave her 30, because she has seven children and her husband is in a mental hospital.

I went over my usual route. I picked up paper, scrap, and rags.

I met a blind man.

"How many years ago did you loose your sight?"

"Ten years."

"Did you find it terrible?"

"No, because everything God does is good."

"What was the reason you went blind?"

"Weakness."

"There was no possibility to cure them?"

"No. Only if they were transplanted. But I needed to find someone who would give me his eyes."

"Then you have seen the sun, the flowers, and the sky filled with stars?"

"I've seen them. Thanks to God."

August 6 Today is José Carlos' birthday. Nine years old. He was born in 1950. What a good age! But he wishes he were ten, because he wants to make love to Clarinda.

I went out and took Vera with me. I picked up paper and found a pair of shoes in the garbage. I sold them for 20 cruzeiros. I bought a half kilo of meat. I cut a slice and had lunch.

August 7 I picked two sacks full of paper and earned 45 cruzeiros. I was desperate. What was I going to do with 45 cruzeiros? I got a few rags and went back to the junk yard to sell them and earned 33 cruzeiros. I was undecided, wondering what to make to eat. I was washing the dishes when there was a knock at the door. José Carlos said:

"It's Dona Teresinha Becker!"

She gave me 500 cruzeiros. I told her that I would buy shoes for José Carlos and thanked her. I accompanied her to her automobile. I went to talk to Chica and showed her the 500 cruzeiros and told her that Dona Teresinha is my white mother.

August 8 A boy died here in the favela. The burial was at 9. The Negroes that accompanied the body rented a truck and took a guitar, a tambourine, and *pinga*. Zirico said:

"When a Japanese dies, the living sing. So we're going to sing too."

The deadliest curse of the favela is the thief. They steal at night and sleep during the day. If I was a man I would not let my children live in this miserable hole. If God helps me to get out of here, I'll never look behind me.

August 12   I cleaned myself up and went to get Vera's money. Senhor Luiz loaned me three cruzeiros. I found one in my pocket, so I had four. I wanted to go on the bus, met a very good *favelado,* and asked to borrow one cruzeiro. He gave me two. I went on the bus.

It was raining and I don't have an umbrella. In the city I heard the people complaining about the lack of beans. That the merchants are hoarding the product from the public so the future price will be higher.

This is not a world for a poor man to live in.

When I got to the Welfare, Senhor J.A.M.V., the father of Vera, had not sent the money.

The father of Vera always begs me not to put his name in the newspapers. That he has many employees and doesn't want his name gossiped around. But he doesn't contribute for me to hide his name. He lives very well and only gives Vera 250 cruzeiros. He only comes around when I appear in the newspapers. He wants to find out how much I earn.

August 13   I got up at 6 a.m. I was furious with life and with a desire to cry because I didn't have money to buy bread. The boys went to school. I went out alone. I left Vera because it was going to rain. I picked up rags and got some cardboard. I earned 30 cruzeiros. I was unhappy thinking: What can 30 cruzeiros buy? I was hungry. I had a cup of coffee and a piece of sweet roll and went back to the favela. When I arrived, Vera was in the window, looking at the cameras of the Vera Cruz Studio that came to film "Promessinha, the Young Bandit." I saw many people watching the scenes. I went to see. When I arrived the vagabonds said:

"Look at Elizabeth Taylor!"

"Go make fun of the Devil!"

I returned and heated some food for the children. Rice and fish. The rice and fish didn't go very far. The children ate and were still hungry. I thought:

"If Jesus Christ would only multiply these fish!"

Senhor Manuel came over. He gave me 200 cruzeiros, but I didn't want to take them.

"Don't you want me any more?"

"I have a lot of things to do. I can't be bothered with men. My one desire is to buy a decent house for my children. I never was lucky with men. That's why I never loved anyone. The men who passed through my life only complicated it more. They left me with children to raise."

He took back the 200 cruzeiros, said good-by, and went away.

I washed the dishes. Later I went to the junk yard to sell scrap iron and rags. I got 21 cruzeiros.

I went to watch the filming of "Promessinha, the Young Bandit." I asked the names of the directors of the film so I could put them in my diary. The women of the favela asked me:

"Carolina, is it true that they are going to tear down the favela?"

"No. They're making a set for a movie."

What I have noticed is that nobody likes the favela, but they need it. I looked at the dread stamped on the faces of the *favelados*.

"They are filming the exploits of Promessinha. But Promessinha wasn't from our favela."

When the actors went to lunch, the *favelados* wanted to break in and take their food. If they only could! Chickens, meat pies, roasts, beer . . . I admired the elegance of the Vera Cruz artists. It is a national Brazilian movie company. It deserves special consideration. They stayed all day in the favela. The favela was overcrowded, and the neighbors from the brick houses were complaining that the intellectuals were favoring the *favelados*.

The people watching the filming made such a racket. Handsome went to see too. I asked him if he had made a film, because he is a singer.

"No, because I'm not famous."

August 15 The women cursed the artists:

"These tramps come here to dirty our door."

People passing on Dutra Street, seeing the fire trucks, come in to see if there is a fire or someone drowning. The people are saying:

"They are filming Promessinha!"

But the title of the film is "Threatened City."

August 16 I spent the afternoon writing. I washed all the clothes. Today I'm happy.

There is a party in the shack of a *nortista*. The favela is overcrowded with *nortistas*. That Orlando Lopes is walking through the favela. He wants money. He charges for electricity on the black market. And there are people in the favela who are starving.

August 26 The worst thing in the world is to go hungry!

December 31 I got up at 3:30 and went to get water. I woke the children and they had their coffee. We went out. João was looking for paper because he wanted money to go to the movies. What torment it is to carry three sacks of paper. We earned 80 cruzeiros. I gave 30 to João.

I went shopping because tomorrow is the first day of the new year. I bought rice, soap, kerosene, and sugar.

João and Vera went to bed. I stayed up writing. Sleep came on me and I slept. I awoke with the whistle of the factory announcing the New Year. I thought of the São Silvestre races and of Manoel de Faria. I asked God to make him win the race. I also asked him to bless Brazil.

I hope that 1960 will be better than 1959. We suffered so much in 1959, that the people were singing:

> "Go! Go for good!
> I don't want you any more.
> No, never more."

January 1, 1960 I got up at 5 and went to get water.

Women's Studies From MENTOR and SIGNET

(0451)

☐ **WOMAN IN SEXIST SOCIETY: Studies in Power and Power-lessness edited by Vivian Gornick and Barbara K. Moran.** Original work by anthropologists, sociologists, historians, literary critics, psychologists, artists, philosophers, and educators on every aspect of the women's liberation movement. "So full of new facts and moving insights, so reasoned, so free from rancor, so uniformly intelligent, that it makes for totally absorbing reading ... the best try to date at undermining the conventional wisdom about women."— *Minneapolis Star.* (618831—$2.50)

☐ **THE EXPERIENCE OF THE AMERICAN WOMAN: 30 Stories edited by Barbara H. Solomon.** The American woman as she appears in American fiction from the first Victorian rebellion against conventional stereotypes to the most open manifestations of liberation today. Includes 30 stories by Kate Chopin, John Updike, Wright Morris, Jean Stafford, Tillie Olsen, Joyce Carol Oates, and others. (621158—$3.95)

☐ **DAUGHTERS & MOTHERS, MOTHERS & DAUGHTERS by Signe Hammer.** The first in-depth psychological study of the relationship between mothers and daughters examining the sex roles played by three generations of women. "Shows us how daughters do or do not free themselves emotionally from their mothers and thus shape their lives ... a first. A must!"—Psychologist Lucy Freeman.

(087216—$1.75)

☐ **A MARY WOLLSTONECRAFT READER edited and with an Introduction by Barbara H. Solomon and Paula S. Berggren.** This anthology of work by the great 18th century feminist, activist, and political philosopher includes excerpts from *A Vindication of the Rights of Men; A Vindication of the Rights of Women;* selections from her letters; the autobiographical *Mary, a Fiction;* the preface to her recently rediscovered pseudonymous work *The Female Reader;* and the complete text of *The Wrongs of Woman, or Maria.* Headnotes. Biographical data. Suggestions for further reading. Bibliography. Index. (621956—$3.95)

Buy them at your local bookstore or use this convenient coupon for ordering.
THE NEW AMERICAN LIBRARY, INC.,
P.O. Box 999, Bergenfield, New Jersey 07621
Please send me the books I have checked above. I am enclosing $_____
(please add $1.00 to this order to cover postage and handling). Send check or money order—no cash or C.O.D.'s. Prices and numbers are subject to change without notice.
Name_____
Address_____
City _____ State _____ Zip Code _____
Allow 4-6 weeks for delivery.
This offer is subject to withdrawal without notice.